MAKE SOMEONE HAPPY
Favorite Postings

Elizabeth Berg

A *W*RITING *M*ATTERS PUBLICATION

ISBN: 978-1-530-56705-8

Author's Website: www.elizabeth-berg.net

Book Design by Phyllis Florin

There are books in which the footnotes or comments scrawled by some reader's hand in the margin are more interesting than the text. The world is one of those books.

-George Santayana

Introduction

When I was an oversensitive teenager, I spent
plenty of time hunched over my desk at home,
filling up pages in a notebook that ended up
becoming my first journal. I wrote about things
that hurt or bedeviled or mystified me, but I also
wrote about things that moved me or made me
laugh or filled me with gratitude and joy. I wrote
about things that might in other people's eyes be
mundane or unimportant but that to me were
little miracles, things that made me feel, as poet
Robert Frost said, that "earth's the right place for
love." And I was always struck by the fact that
even if I were writing about things that made me
sad, the relief of putting those things on the page
made me happy, in the way that a good cry may
not solve the problem but at least allows getting
something out that *needs* out.

Years after I'd became an oversensitive
author who had left journaling far behind, I was
persuaded that it might be a good thing for me to
enter the modern world and establish a website.
This I did, albeit reluctantly. One of the things
on elizabeth-berg.net was a blog, and to my
surprise, I found that I really enjoyed writing it. It
put me back in journal mode, sharing in a rather
casual and unfettered way things that were on my
mind. The pleasure and relief that brought was
the same as what I had felt as a teenager.

Then it seemed the website was not enough,
and I was urged to create a Facebook page. The
bad part was that postings began to take the

place of blogging, but the good part was the kind of interaction with readers that Facebook allowed. I was stunned to find, eventually, that it seemed I had a self-selected community I could turn to for all kinds of things: celebration, commiseration, enlightenment, and the sharing of wonder, of those little miracles.

The way readers embraced these offerings reinforced something I learned well as a nurse: it's always the little things that matter most, that offer the richest meaning, that, above all, make us comfortable, even proud to be, in our own skins: the cup we prefer for coffee in the morning, the dim outline of our dog asleep beside us at night, the plunking sound of the first blueberry into the bucket, the grasping of a finger of our hand by a baby. It made me understand too that to record ordinary life *validates* ordinary life, and also validates us as a struggling species that makes an awful lot of mistakes but is nonetheless full of kindness and caring and hope. And charm, too, especially when we think no one's looking.

More and more often, readers began urging me to have my blog and postings put into book form, a physical object to have and to hold; to, as one reader suggested "take to the beach, or bed, or on an airplane." I thought this was a swell idea. And so I endeavored to collect entries to deliver to you, like flowers to a mailbox.

This book is meant to offer you the particular kind of satisfaction you have told me you experience in having someone put into words what you feel, too. It seems that E.M. Forster is now and forever relevant: what we need most is to connect. When we do, whether in sorrow or in joy or even in befuddlement, we feel better.

Thank you for asking for this book, thereby proving that words matter, and that bound works you can have and hold and line up on your shelf do, too. I hope *Make Someone Happy* makes you happy.

Make Someone Happy

Good Morning!

Everybody has days when we get up on the wrong side of the bed. This was such a day for me. I woke up grumpier than grumpy. So I clomped around for a while, thinking about how I have to go to the stupid doctor today and will have to deal with stupid traffic and so on. Made some stupid coffee. Looked at the sofa where I usually do my morning meditation and sighed. Okay. Got my stupid coffee, went to sit down, and glared straight ahead. What I often do, in these brief meditations, is to think about what's beautiful and right in my life. I thought about my grandchildren, and the indicator needle jumped, but I was still squarely in the land of grumpdom. Then I thought about the fact that I was alive and healthy. Then I took in a deep breath and tried to empty my mind, as they say, tried to look out at nothing, but the cat was in the way. And the cat began scratching the carpet as she is NOT supposed to do, and she KNOWS it. "Gracie!" I said. She immediately stopped scratching and rolled on her back and made her tail curl in a most amazing way. It sort of looked like a question mark. I watched her for a while, all stripes and green eyes and an enviable sense of bonhomie. She began licking her paw in preparation for washing her face, and if THAT hasn't cornered the market on animal cuteness, I don't know what has. Behind Gracie, through the glass doors that lead to the deck, I saw a little flurry of blossoms blow past, a kind of springtime blizzard. I saw a bird on the wire, just like in the song, and the wire swayed in the wind, and the bird cocked its head to the left and the right and stayed on. I saw that the blossoms on the old lilac tree at the yard had pushed open further. I saw a squirrel balanced on top of a very narrow fence and he moved forward without seeming to have any sense at all that he would do anything but stay up and move forward. And here we are. Good morning, emphasis on good.

Decluttering

Yesterday, inspired by all the things I've read about the joy and freedom of decluttering, I began my own journey toward liberation. One project a day, I decided, and I attacked a closet. Out with the darling coat that I never wear, out with jewelry I never wear, out with scarves, etc, etc. There was one thing that gave me pause, and that was the dress my mom wore to her prom and entrusted to me. I've had it for years, the black and white, long, simple dress, with the Chinese-style white silk jacket that I believe her sister gave her to wear over it. The gown is tiny, fragile, and I suppose most people would call it out of date, but I call it vintage, which equals fantastic. I've kept it and kept it, and I know full well that no one will ever wear it or want it, it's just something that once meant a lot to her, and there must be some DNA on there somewhere. But why am I keeping it? I asked myself. There is no reason. It's time to let it go. I gave it a little kiss and decided to take a photo of it. Then I'd still have it, in a way. I filled a box with clothes and folded the dress and the jacket so carefully and lay it on top as though it were a newborn. I thought, maybe, rather than donating it, I should just throw it out. No one is going to want it. In the morning, I told myself. In the morning, when the birds are singing and all hope is alive, I'll throw it out really fast and never look back. This morning, I took it out of the box with the same great care I used in putting it in there. And I marched it right back upstairs and hung it up in the closet and I will keep it forever.

The Danger of Expectations

Last night, I grumbled to a friend that I had to take the dogs out and it was COLD. I hate being cold, and I am the first to admit I'm a big baby about it. I leashed up the dogs, buttoned up my coat to my throat and went outside with my teeth gritted.

Reader, it was not cold.

Behind the houses across the street, I saw the clouds pinkened by dusk, and against a blue and yellow horizon they were so pretty I had to stand still for a moment to take them in. (You can imagine how well this went over with the mutts, who were frantic to get going: so little time, so much to sniff.) We began to walk, and I took in the sight of the leaves, serious now in turning burgundy and gold and lime green and that heart-breakingly beautiful cross of yellow and red that reads as coral.

Halloween decorations are out, and we walked past many a fake cemetery and many spider webs and one scarecrow sitting out on a chair in the yard among headstones and skeletons that I thought would freak Gabby right out, but when I pointed it out to her, saying, "What's that, huh? What's THAT?" (nothing like stirring up trouble, I always say), she said, "What, it's some scarecrow somebody put out. Let's GO."

I thought of all the kids who would soon be traipsing around the neighborhood, some exuberant, some sullen, some so young as to be utterly confused about the whole affair. I hope it's nice weather for them. I hope they get good stuff. I used to stay out for ten thousand hours trick-or-treating and then keep my loot bag by my bed so I could gobble down Milk Duds before sleep. (My dentist was thrilled by this, as you can imagine.)

We walked to the playground and the dusk deepened and then the lights came on in houses, and on the passing cars, and there you go, another day was done. If there is one thing I know about my life, it is that there will never be enough time given over to the glory of nature simply being itself in everyday ways, and to the beauty and poignancy of time passing and to pleasant little thoughts like I wonder who will have homemade costumes this year.

This has been a little homily intended to illustrate the danger of expectations. Because you just never know. You go outside all set to be miserable and come home elated.

Old Dogs

According to the statistics, my older Golden, Homer, has lived past his expiration date. He is twelve. A lot of the time, most of the time, he spends lying on the floor. He is like an alive rug, though he races to his food bowl twice a day, and he trots along amiably on his walks.

But.

The writing is on the wall. Homer's walks have to be shorter, now. He gets up with great difficulty, and often times, his back legs tremble. Climbing steps? Sometimes he makes it up and down, but other times his legs spay out beneath him. Jump in the car? No more. He gazes up at the open gate of my SUV like an old man looking at a faded photo of himself in his prime, flexing.

This morning, Homer was more inactive than usual. He ate, went out, and then lay unmoving for hours, I would check on him now and then, and his tail would flop once, twice, but he would not get up. It is his habit to come into every room I'm in—not right away, but eventually. Not today.

So I was lying on my bed making notes for a novel I want to write (often times, I think better when I'm lying down; maybe it's because the blood doesn't have to work so hard to get to my beleaguered brain), and I kept thinking of Homer, down in the kitchen, alone. I thought, I'm going to go down there with a pillow and a notebook and lie beside him. I know there are some crumbs on the floor, and there are a few scattered feathers from the parakeet in a very pretty shade of blue. Before I sweep them up, it could be interesting to have a close-up view. I could lie right next to Homer and scratch his head while I wrote out ideas. I could talk to him now and then. I could pretend I was at the yoga studio I go to, where, when I lie on the floor, it's spiritual.

So I came down to do that but first I wanted to go out onto the back deck to put some coffee grounds into the potted plants I have there. I did, and then propped the back door open so that Gabby, my four-year-old Golden mix, could go in and out. I sat in one of chairs on the deck for a while, grieving the loss of Homer's abilities but at the same time taking in what is a really nice day: the birds singing, the sky a washed-looking blue, the flowers all bright and healthy and inoffensively show-offy. Then what to my wondering eyes should appear but Homer, coming slowly out onto the deck, too. He stood blinking in the sun, then raised his nose to sniff and sniff at something delectable that was in the air, reading the dog newspaper. And then he lay down as close to me as he could, and I pet him and murmured endearments that would be too embarrassing for me to repeat here and we were both content. And then I realized: Homer is always content. Because he is always accepting. If he has to sleep a lot, so what? If his legs are weak, well, then, his legs are weak. He still enjoys his life. He does not ask for more.

They say, probably erroneously, that you can't teach an old dog new tricks. But an old dog can certainly teach his people some.

Playground Bulletin No. 1

Yesterday I was walking through the playground when I saw a young boy maybe nine or ten come over to the slide and then stand on it like a low-key king of the hill. He just stood there, unmoving. I was very interested in what he might be doing but I didn't want to stare directly at him, so I sat on a nearby bench and busied myself petting my dog. The boy walked up the slide; then, knees bent, carefully walked back down. I thought suddenly, "he's killing time waiting for a friend." As if on cue, his friend appeared, another young boy about the same age wearing shorts, a t-shirt and Clark Kent black glasses. Mr. Spectacles had a high voice like a girl; the other boy had a very low voice. They sat on another bench and discussed the whereabouts of other friends who hadn't shown up at what I gathered was their meeting place. High and low, high and low, they speculated as to what might have happened. Mr. Spectacles said he thought they'd been scared off by the rain, and the disdain for such cowardly behavior didn't even need to be discussed: it was all there in the boys' crossed arms. I left before I could hear what the alternate plans might have been, but I'll tell you something: if those boys had said "Hey, lady, we're going to go and catch some minnows, want to come?" I would have been speechless with joy. As it is, maybe I'll get my own mason jar and find a creek alive with minnows and catch a few and watch them for a while before I set them free again. Sometimes I think that everything I did when I was nine years old is superior to everything I've done since.

 *Gabby*

Gabby is one of my dogs, a Golden/Springer Spaniel mix. She likes to weigh in every now and then.

Gabby: Yesterday I heard you tell someone my fans were becoming legion.

Me: Yes. Are you glad?

Gabby: Depends. What does "legion" mean?

Me: Many. Lots.

Gabby: LEGION means that?

Me: Yes.

Gabby: That doesn't make any sense. "Legion" should mean walking stick. Or it should be the name of chewing tobacco. Then you could say, "Did you bring your legion?" and the guy could wave his stick in the air or pat his pocket and say, "Right here!" Legion could be a name for a car, too. Or a hospital.

Me: My, aren't you full of suggestions?

Gabby: If you want a word that means "lots of" why don't you say something like "hoggo" or "whoasome." She has hoggo fans.

Me: We'll see if we can't work it into the lexicon.

Gabby: I know you want to go to work. But I want to tell you one more thing. You know when you took me to Five Guys with you yesterday? Why did you tie me to the post outside like a burro to a hitching post? By the way, "burro" means "ass." And that's how I felt.

Me: I had to tie you up while I went in to get our order. If you were loose you might have been hit by a car or gotten lost.

Gabby: Yeah, but if I WEREN'T hit by a car or lost, I would have come right back!

Me: Sorry. You have to get tied up sometimes.

Gabby: At least you shared your fries.

Me: And I wiped the salt off for you. And then I kissed you on your snout right in front of everyone.

Gabby: Yes. You know how you say "Stay," to me sometimes?

Me: Yes?

Gabby: I want to say that to you, too.

Me: Well, when I say "stay" I mean don't move.

Gabby: Well, when I say it, I mean never leave.

Me: I won't.

Gabby: Me neither. Now get to work. I'm almost out of treats.

Kindness

The "latest" mass killing, I read in the paper. As though it's a fashion trend. For me, there is only one way to think of this, only one hope to have. And that is for each person to look into his or her own heart and mind to find a way to see others as precious and irreplaceable. Others and themselves, too. Because acts like these come from people who have no self-love.

Each small deed we do can add up to something. Each small deed can become a practice that has a wider effect than we may think. Kindness inspires kindness. Letting a car go ahead of you in traffic. Saying please and thank you as a general practice. Using good manners on the phone, at the grocery store. Listening to points of view that may be different from your own with an open heart and mind, and working toward a compromise that is best for all. Being gentle. Understanding that coolness and irony can only go so far (which is to say not very far at all) in trying to create a place where we all feel safe and cared for.

Each day, we have the opportunity to step outside and begin. Each day we have the opportunity to recognize that the change for good can happen one deed and one individual at a time, and each day we can make a solemn promise to do our part. It's hard to do; we're human, but it's never been more necessary to try. You know the song: *Let there be peace on earth, and let it begin with me.* Peace to you, and I wish you many small joys on another day that we are privileged to have on this bruised but still beautiful earth. Another day that we cannot take for granted, and never could.

Baby Birds

It is all I can do to tear myself away from my back porch. From there, I can see mother and father robin taking turns feeding their babies. There are two babies, and when they hear the rustle of their parents' wings, their heads pop up, their beaks open wide and that is exactly how they stay, excluding the time they take to swallow. I find something so heartening about all of this: the way the babies are fed, the way that, during the rainstorm (and then hailstorm!) that we had the other day, the mother sat resolutely on top of her children, protecting them. She will feed them and protect them and then the day will come when she will see them fly away.

It is what we do with our own children, of course, only we get to stay in touch. We get to have grandchildren, if we're lucky. I know I have a problem with anthropomorphizing, but how I wish those birds would get together for reunions with the baby birds of their baby birds. (I was going to say get together for Thanksgiving, but how horrifying to envision the birds gathered together around a table where a roasted bird is being served! "White meat or dark?" the host would ask, and the guest would swallow and say, "Um, neither?")

Aging

I have been thinking a lot about what aging means, as I suppose a lot of people who are aging do. We think about it and we fret about it and we don't all that often celebrate it. But today I picked up a book by philosopher, essayist and poet George Santayana and opened it to this sentence: "Old age is the time for happiness." A bit later, making an initial attempt to clean up the files on my computer, I came across an essay I'd written about aging, part of which I will share with you now, as a kind of echo to Santayana's words...

And then there are the little surprises, things that get left out of the handbook due to their relative unimportance. These are the paper cuts of aging; they are minor, yes; but they are annoying. And they hurt more than you'd think.

You go to put on your cute ballet flats and they don't fit any more: your feet have heard the clarion call for your body to spread out, and they have gotten bigger. Also their topography has changed. So long toe cleavage, hello bunions. Bunions! The very word is enough to make you put down your fork. You might as well add the word "gumption" to your vocabulary. Or how about this: You enter into a certain mood and look up an old flame on Facebook. What you find is that he's old, all right. Popular music is not your music, and you don't recognize most of the people in *People*.

There is something else that comes with aging, and that is the particular kind of loneliness it brings. Even if you live with other people, there comes a day of private reckoning when you see that you must rely upon yourself for your deepest needs. There is no Prince Charming. You are the princess and the prince.

So, yes, aging brings things that are hard to deal with. But it also brings things we are blessed to have. Your appreciation of time increases. When you were a kid, a summer day lasted eons. Not any more. Now you recognize time's swift passage and all that implies. It is bittersweet, but the emphasis is on sweet. Thus it is that you are standing in a shaft of sunlight, peeling an apple, and everything becomes illuminated, inside and out, because you have finally learned to be in the moment. You see the beauty in a cluster of apple seeds, in the ribs of a sliced-open green pepper, in the lime green stripe at the base of a slice of watermelon.

When ego steps aside—as aging demands— you are better able to enter into altruism because you are looking past yourself. You may find yourself wanting to pass on and provide for. You may come to understand that not only are your family and friends worthy of care and attention, the whole world is, because it turns out that the whole world is your family, too. And if you embrace that concept, your compassion can grow like Jack's beanstalk. You can happily abandon your fantasies of being everlastingly young and rich and famous and understand that true wealth and beauty have nothing to do with money or good looks. Your legacy can be simple and clear: I was here, and I cared, and I showed it.

 *Gabby*

Gabby: Did you get me my Christmas present yet?

Me: ....What?

Gabby: Did you get me my Christmas present yet?

Me: Why would I do that? It's not Christmas time.

Gabby: It isn't? I thought it was Christmas time.

Me: Why?

Gabby: It's COLD like Christmas.

Me: You're right. But it's May.

Gabby: What's May?

Me: A month in the middle of the year.

Gabby: Oh. I don't go by that. I go by other things, because of my superior brain, no offense. You know: scent. Instinct. Temperature. But listen, I have to go out. Should I go and stand beneath my leash so you get the message? Or perhaps turn in circles really, really fast?

Me: No. Come on, let's go.

Gabby: Maybe when we're out, you can buy me my Christmas present.

Joy

We have arrived at that curious time of year when spring seems to have come, but not really. I leave the kitchen door open to hear the birds. The crocuses are up, and the crayon-colored tulips won't be far behind. Buds are swelling on the trees. The air is milder, and not too many jackets are fully zipped—this is the time of year when you see kids "wearing" their coats by placing hoods over their heads and that's that. But the lawns aren't green yet, and in the absence of the white of snow, things look a little dirty and despairing. Still, if there is anything that living through a hard winter teaches us, it's that when spring really does come, in all its blossomy glory, we who have suffered are the ones most capable of enjoying the resurrection. In a way, it reminds me of that old adage: no joy like joy after sorrow.

 *Gabby*

All morning, I struggled to fix my FB page, which wasn't letting me post. Sweated BULLETS so I could FIX it so I could POST. And now I find I have nothing to say.

Gabby: I do! I do!

Me: Later.

Gabby: That's your favorite word.

A Writer's Life

People ask if I like going out on book tour. And I say yes and no. I love meeting other authors I admire. I love meeting people who read my books and often have wonderful, bolstering things to say to me. I love room service breakfast. I love seeing my books in stores all over the country. I always go and stand before them and say, sotto voce, "You okay?" and they always say, "Yes. Stop blocking us from view. We are TRYING to WORK here."

I don't like airports, unless there are little kids hauling brightly colored little suitcases behind them, bonus points for teddy bears strapped onto them. I don't like not having the grounding experiences of chatting daily with people in stores and on the streets of my 'hood. I miss the sanctuary quality of home.

The publication of a new book can make a writer feel a little wobbly. Out on tour, she can end up sitting on the edge of a hotel bed wishing hard that her dog was there sighing out its nose, because that simple sound brings great comfort, as does the regular tick-tock of the clock on her mantle, as does the sight of the steps leading up to her own front porch. A new book means a writer becomes subject to subjectivity: she reads favorable reviews and nearly blushes; she reads not so favorable ones and despairs.

But a writer is blessed to be published, and even more blessed to able to go out on tour, and so it falls to her to buck up, to load her heart and soul with things that soothe her and make her feel stronger. She carries a hanky in her purse that belonged to her mother. She carries a card in her suitcase that her grandson wrote to her. She brings a little light-up bird to put in hotel rooms to glow in the night. And she is grateful for certain acts of serendipity such as the following quote, read by her this morning, that offered exactly what she was looking for today: from Patricia Hampl's "To the Reader" in *I Could Tell You Stories*: *"A writer is, first and last, a reader. Who do you write for, Gertrude Stein was asked, and famously replied, 'Myself and strangers.' That self, the reader self who is allied with strangers, may be a writer's better half, more detached, more trustworthy, than the writing self who swaggers through a lifetime of prose. It is difficult—and diminishing—to separate the self who writes from the one who reads. Both acts belong to the communion of the word, which is a writer's life."*

Hotel Amenity

I love the hotel I'm staying in, not because of its glorious sheets or thick towels or good coffee, but because outside the building is an opossum with three babies. The mother is backed into a shady corner and the babies are tucked under her. The babies are curious—you see their tiny heads popping out now and then, and when they do, I am helpless against a kind of clasped-hands delight. Find me a person who is not enchanted by the genius of genetics, the miniaturization of form. The mother is standing guard, and it seems to me that her face shows a little fear, but also defiance: *I am NOT moving.* When I came upon her, I watched her for a while, and I spoke gently to her, telling her that she and her babies would be all right (hoping they would be) and hoping too that no one would bother or frighten her by trying to take her picture, everybody has to take a picture of everything these days and post it on Facebook. Then I went up to my room for a while. Then I came back down and tried to take her picture so I could post it on Facebook. Luckily for her, I have no idea how my new phone camera works, so it was a bust. But there she still was, I was relieved to see, with her white face and pink nose, and with her babies safe. I love how opossums look both familiar and exotic. And I love that there you are, just minding your own business, and suddenly you get a live greeting card from nature.

Playground Bulletin No. 2

A report from the playground on the first nice day in a thousand years (or so it seems): Today the kids' jackets are off and lie on the ground like fabric puddles, except for one boy who has his jacket wrapped around his head like a turban. The girls have taken over the swings, and they lean their heads back as far as their necks will let them as they pump ever higher. There are three girls who have very strange hairdos: knots of hair gathered up here and there in messy clumps, the rest of the hair hanging down. It looks like one little girl did it as a joke to another little girl, then female solidarity kicked in and now they have undoubtedly started a fad—this is, after all, the hometown of Tavi Gevinson.

Suddenly a memory flashes into my head: me as a senior in high school starting to leave the house wearing white lipstick. "What's that on your mouth?" my Dad asks. I tell him. He makes a face. It's 1965, Twiggy is big, and so is white lipstick. "Everyone's wearing it," I say. "Take it off," he says, and I do. And not all that resentfully, either, since secretly I think he's right: those of us who have adopted this fad look like corpses.

Also on the playground this morning are five girls doing handstands in a circle, and you can see a few bellybuttons. One little boy, maybe eight or nine, has had the foresight to wear sunglasses today, and he is walking around like the inspector general. Off on the playing field are a large group of boys with a soccer ball. One says, "Whoo-hoo!" seemingly at nothing. Well, I guess he's saying it to the day. As am I.

Real People

I am home before I set out on tour again tomorrow. I really need a butler to pack for me, because I always forget something. Once, it was pajamas, and I slept in the hotel bathrobe, which was so uncomfortable. I know, I know; you're thinking, why didn't you just sleep nude? Here's why: because if there had been a fire, surely I would have panicked and run into the hall naked, which might have been okay forty years ago but now would only add distress to an already distressed population.

So many lovely things happened this last week. I got to see how passages read aloud from my book were received by Real People, and I got to hear endless praise because of course on tour people don't come up and say to your face, "I really hated your book. Ew." (Although one author told me someone came up to him at a signing and said, "I really like your books. But not this one.") To this person, I would like to send "Miss Elizabeth's Guide to Manners, Duh."

One woman brought me a wrist corsage—for the second time, as she pointed out. "Oh, I love wrist corsages!" I told her. "I know," she said. "You told me that last time" "I always wanted one to wear to the prom, but I never got one," I said, and she said, "I know, You told me that last time, too." I snapped that corsage right on and I felt like Principessa Elizabetta.

Blessings

This is a tale of polka dots, possibilities, and pliés.

This morning, when I opened the shutters of my study, I saw a little girl, maybe four years old, walking down the sidewalk in a sparkly white tutu. Cute, I thought, and turned to my work. When I looked up again, there was another little girl in a tutu. Soon they were everywhere, like the annual swarming of Monarch butterflies, and I beheld them in that way, too: nice enough to see one monarch, but when you see them SWARMing..... I noticed that the ballerinas were gathered at the elementary school at the end of my street, along with many parents and grandparents, many of whom held flowers that I presumed would be given to the performers.

"Dance recital?" I asked, and a mother smiled and said, "Yes."

I went in to see if I could buy a ticket. "We're oversold," a young girl told me, "but you can go in and have a peek." I went in, and never have I seen an audience smiling so much and so obviously happy to be there. In addition to the adults in the audience, there were the siblings of the performers, some young ones with pacifiers casually hanging out of their mouth just in case they REALLY needed them, some long-suffering older brothers, some babies, one of whom was cross-eyed in his very serious investigation of his father's collar. There was a little stunner around five years old in a polka dot dress and fancy shoes, there was a little girl in a pink sweatshirt of around ten with obvious disabilities who was greeted warmly and affectionately by many and she greeted them right back in the same way.

The show was made up of a few acts, opening with a dance by very little girls to the beginning of "Swan Lake." They moved their arms most gracefully, as if they were trying in a pretty way for lift-off while they ran around in a circle, trying succcessfully for the most part not to bump into one another. To the music of "Carmen Suite No. 1," there was a drama involving a little boy who brandished a long sword and at one point ran between rows of the ballerinas making a kind of tunnel by linking their hands high up. The only problem was, they forgot to stand far apart, so that when the boy with the sword had to run down the tunnel it was like he was hacking his way through a forest of tulle. The final number that I saw was set to The Andrew Sisters' "Sing, Sing, Sing." If that song doesn't get your toes tapping, your foot is glued to the floor. The little girls were dressed as sailors and they were tap dancing, and if there's one thing I like it's tap dancing. Also sailors, but I'm kind of past that now. Kind of. Not all the way.

So.

A glance out the window, and I got to enjoy such a sweet show. And now the day continues to be good: the weather fine, people out sweeping cut grass from sidewalks, shaking rugs, sitting in lawn chairs to watch their children play and to remember the unadulterated joy of sitting in the Big Room known as outside. Did you ever notice how

everything tastes better when you eat it outside?
Robins are hopping around swell-breasted, dogs
are trotting just a little more joyfully along. Winter
is over; spring has finally sprung. We feel
confident enough to say it out loud, with a kind of
pride, as if we are responsible for the change in
weather. (A-yup, finally got 'er going!) Sometimes
blessings are little. Sometimes they're big. And
sometimes they're both at the same time.

Connections

I am aware of the irony of using the internet to complain about the internet, but here I go. My gripe du jour is that I learn something, or download something, and then it changes. And then I have to download something else and I try to, and it doesn't work, and soon I have all these little downloads having babies, you know, the xxx1, xxx2, xxx3, but nothing *works*.

I feel sometimes like I'm being bullied by people I can't see who make arbitrary decisions about things that I don't necessarily agree with; that changes are being made for change's sake. I feel that I'm being pushed into using a new version of blah blah blah and I don't know why. And I don't know where to go to get help. To the Apple store? To a consulting service, where I will have to admit that I'm not so very sure that I know what "browser" REALLY means, that to me it sounds like a modification of a pretty good dog name and nothing else?

I get overwhelmed with all this stuff. Just now, after trying to download a new version of Adobe, I had to give up and go and lie down on the sofa and look out the window. I imagined a little house like the kind children draw, with flowers in a window box and fat puffs of smoke coming out of a chimney and green grass standing up straight and neat as a crew cut. I wanted to open the paper door and go into the paper house and live there because I imagined that even though it was pretend, everything in it would be real. Virtual is not welcome in my life anymore. Same with multitasking and sound bites and Twitter. Here is what is welcome in my life: Depth. Reflection. The ability to pay attention to one thing at a time so as to see it wholly. Kindness. Connection. And chicken potpie.

One Butterfly on One Rose

Last night, I saw the movie "Still Alice." Afterwards, I needed to be quiet for a pretty long time. I kept thinking about a line in the movie (and if you haven't seen it, I don't think this will spoil anything for you). The line came soon after Alice's diagnosis of early-onset Alzheimer's when she says, "I wish I had cancer." I immediately thought, I'll bet a lot of people with catastrophic cancer diagnoses would say, "I wish I had Alzheimer's." Maybe any of us with a grim prognosis would look over any fence and say, Boy, it sure seems greener over there.

When I was a nurse, I took care of an older woman whose name was Jenny, and she had Alzheimer's. I once took a bouquet of flowers she had sitting at her bedside to the nearby utility room to freshen up the water in the large vase. When I brought the bouquet back to her room, she gasped in pleasure and said, "Oh, look! Someone sent me flowers!" And I thought, well, maybe it's not all bad having Alzheimer's.

My dad got Alzheimer's before he died, and when I visited him toward the end, I would sit at the little kitchen table with him and he would ask the same question over and over, and over and over I would answer it like it was the first time he had asked it: Here's your bouquet, here's your bouquet, here's your bouquet.

Before I went to sleep last night, I finished reading Rachel Joyce's lovely novel, "The Love Song of Miss Queenie Hennessy." Queenie is in a hospice, and her medical problems are many and, in some respects, lurid. She has her moments of despair. But mostly she fills her life with love: of fellow patients and of caregivers, of the movement of leaves on the trees outside, of memories, of her own evolving journey.

I wish sometimes that we could all keep uppermost in our minds that our time here is short at the longest. But it seems that none of us can do that. We get bogged down in minutiae, and in hatred, in love, in greed and ambition and confusion and desire and hope and joy and in every other thing that makes us the imperfect and spectacular beings that we are. We lose sight of the big picture, which makes us best able to appreciate the small picture. One butterfly on one rose. And then, a petal on the rose.

I am at an age where life begins to reverse itself: a body tearing down rather than building up. A mind not quite so quick as it was—not that it was THAT quick at its quickest. But still.

I recently talked to someone ninety-two years old who was struggling with depression and was chiding herself for feeling that way. I said, "Well, why wouldn't you feel depressed, facing the losses you've dealt with? It must be hard." And then, right when I was going to follow that with something along the lines of "You know what, though? There were five male cardinals in my back yard this morning!" she said, "I guess I'll get out and socialize more." I felt like cheering.

I don't know. At any age, what can we do but go and rest our arms along the top of the fence and talk to everyone else? Even if we limp out there. Even if we are pushed, or carried, and even if we just look out the window to see others gathered together, in solidarity of the rarest, richest kind.

Benny

It is my unfortunate habit to pay more attention to dogs that walk past my window than to the people who are walking them. (The exception is if the walker is a kid; then interest levels in the dog and the human are equal.) For many years, I've been watching Benny, the Goldendoodle who lives across the street from me. He's what I'd call avuncular, he has an air of dogly kindness that exceeds the usual level, he's kind of an old soul dog, and his tail is always wagging. He looks like he has a bad perm, but he's handsome nonetheless, and just the right size, if you're a person who prefers big dogs.

Benny got old too fast, as dogs do. (Next time God's looking over his punch list, I hope he fixes that.) He got old, and then older, and then he lost his sight and his hearing and then he lost his ability to climb up and down the stairs that lead into his house. Sometimes I would look out the window and see his owner carrying him up the steps and my heart would ache and then I would remember that Benny still wags his tail as he walks slowly along, still sniffs the ground and the bushes and the trees with the pleasure of a baron sniffing brandy. I would remind myself not to decide for Benny whether his life was good or not, since his view of his own doings seemed to be perpetually on the side of enormous satisfaction. Nonetheless, I bought a so-sorry-your-dog-died card to have at the ready. And then I watched Benny out the window almost every day, still being Benny.

Finally, I threw the card away, thinking it might be bad juju to have it around.

One day I was in George's coffee shop having a feta cheese and spinach omelet when I saw Benny's owner, who was just leaving George's. She came up to me and we exchanged pleasantries. She sold her house, she told me—last time I saw her, she said she was trying to sell it.

"Oh, congratulations," I said, and she smiled. "How's Benny?" I asked next, and her eyes filled with tears. And my eyes filled with tears. I got up and hugged her and said, "I'm so sorry," and she nodded. I said thickly, "I loved so much watching him, with his nose to the ground and his tail wagging. He was such a nice dog." She nodded again, taking in my little eulogy.

"He got so that he couldn't...we brought him to the vet, and the vet started to cry and said, 'He is not the same dog; he's in pain; you have to put him down.' So someone came to the house and we were all with him...."

Now we were both actively crying. I told her again how sorry I was and then I kind of desperately changed the subject so we could both stop crying and then she left and I finished my omelet and it was very good and I left the waitress a big tip. And outside the sun was shining and the planet was spinning, and hyacinths were sleeping in the earth and babies were being born, and puppies.

I thought, the only good thing about sorrow is that it brings us down to ground zero inside ourselves, it reacquaints us with our best and truest self, and it releases compassion like some mighty hormone and if there is one thing that is good for us, it's to have compassion, because it brings us together. I know my neighbor's heart feels like it's up against the cheese grater. But I know she will heal. And I hope that whoever lives across the street from her next will get to see her carrying a dog up the stairs again, only this time it will be because his puppy legs are too short. Soon, though, he will be bounding down those stairs, and up.

Libraries

Yesterday, I had the great privilege of talking to librarians about *The Dream Lover*. I have loved libraries since I was a little girl and was brought to them by my mother, who used to plow through library books like I go through a box of Sees chocolates, which is to say with great speed and pleasure. I used to like to play with the card catalogue: as I told the librarians, I would pull out the long drawers and rifle professionally through those elegantly typed cards, never mind that I couldn't read yet. I rifled through the cards and pretended I was wearing high heels and red lipstick and that I was WORKING at my JOB. Soon, I got my own library card and it seemed a miracle to me that I could go and get as many books as I wanted—for free. It still does seem that way. Libraries have changed a lot since the days when I first went to them—long gone, alas, are the little half pencil/half stampers that were once used when you checked out books. But the other day I was at my library sitting in a spot of sunshine at a big wooden table with a high stack of reference books and I was happy as a clam. All around me were people engaged in using this wonderful space in different ways, and all of us, I think, were grateful to be in what I think of as a Common Church.

So when I met a librarian yesterday who told me they had tried to close her branch but it's being kept open by volunteers, I wanted to do a triple flip. Unfortunately, I cannot now and never could do even one flip. I suppose I could have attempted a cartwheel, but why invite tragedy to triumph?

Queen for a Day

It's hard to think there's any sentient being who doesn't understand the charm of reading to young children. Their guileless acceptance of the story. The sound of their breathing. The warm weight of them on your lap or beside you. The things they choose to comment on, or ask questions about. The way, when they point at a picture, you see the size of their fingernails. How their lovies are often tucked under their arms so that they can hear the stories, too.

But the last time I was going to read to my just-turned-six-year-old grandson, Danny, I decided to change things up a bit. "You read to me," I said. Danny can't read yet, but since when has a challenge kept a good man down? He took up a random book, and "read" this to me: "Once there was a woman who didn't live her life. And her age was zero." I thought, Whoa, if you really think of it, that's deep. He's talking about what happens when you don't self-actualize. He's talking about how we all need to stay open to learning life lessons. I wanted to ask him if he was the reincarnation of the Buddha, but I was afraid he'd look me right in the eye and calmly say, "Yes." So I just said, "REEEEallllly?" and he said "Yes!" and then he giggled that little boy giggle and my contentment level jumped like on the applause meter on the old Queen for a Day show. I used to beg my mom to go on that show. She never would entertain the notion. I couldn't understand why anyone would pass up the opportunity to be WHISKED away. I kind of still don't.

Winter

Many of you posted today to speak of the beauties of winter in the face of my complaining about it. As I write this, the sky has reddened at the horizon, and the black branches of trees are standing out against the dimming light. The snow is almost glowing. Lights are beginning to come on in the neighborhood. I have a big pot of chicken soup on the stove and just the smell of it is therapeutic. This afternoon I bought new flannel sheets. All of which is to say I am so very comfortable, and grateful that I am. And I want to revise my earlier statement. I don't hate winter. I hate being cold. And even then, I can tolerate a bit of it so long as I know I can come inside quickly and feel warmth settle around me like a king's mantle. Thank you for reminding me that it's never the thing; rather, it's the way you look at it.

Lucky Ones

Again, I woke up to horrible news of a bombing in the Middle East. I heard a man saying, "I lost everything..." I wondered that he was able to speak. The local traffic report came on next, and it seemed obscene to me. I made coffee, I sat in my customary spot in my customary way to read a poem and then give myself over to ten minutes of stillness and a search for gratitude. It was hard for me to learn to do this. I had to start with setting the timer for a few minutes and force myself not to leap up to straighten a picture or get more coffee or answer the phone, but now I come to this practice every day with relief and with the knowledge that it will water something essential in me that otherwise has a tendency to dry up.

Sitting in reverie today, I began by feeling such deep sadness for the ever-escalating violence and ignorance and fear in the world, but I ended with something different, which is the realization that my despair will do those who suffer no good at all. It falls to those of us who happen to be lucky at the moment to hold onto joy, to try to spread it, to serve in that way as some sort of necessary balance. Sometimes we are the children who come to their mothers for comfort, and sometimes we are the mothers who offer that comfort to others. It's a lesson I learned long ago, working as a nurse, which I guess I needed to relearn today. You don't come to the bed of a suffering patient with his suffering on your own face. You come bringing whatever you can of an internal light. You sit right on the bed, never mind the mandate you learned in school not to have such intimate contact. You sit on the bed and you take up a hand and you make sure you really look and really listen and really touch—hand to hand, spirit to spirit, heart to heart.

Why Worry?

My Golden, Homer, is twelve and a half, and Bill and I worry about him all the time: his slow gait, his great difficulty getting up from a lying down position, his worsening hearing, his poor vision—he often uses his nose for his eyes, sniffing rather than looking to see who's there.

Last night, I was lying in bed reading, and I heard a kind of thumping sound. Then here came Gabby, our five year old Golden, up the stairs, looking a bit distressed. Then she began to tremble, and I realized she was having a seizure. She has them every now and then, and I've learned that the best thing to do is just hold her and talk soothingly to her. When the seizure was over, it took just a minute for her to come back to herself; then she went over to the window to look out, wagging her tail at every passer-by. Not so much for me: I had gotten leg cramps when I was holding her and I was having my own difficulty getting up off the floor. When Bill came home, I told him about Gabby, and he got that sad look he always gets when any animal suffers, or seems to. We talked about the pets for a while, and then Bill got up to go and get something and he was limping. "What's wrong with your leg?" I asked. "Nothing," he said. "Your foot?" I asked. "Nah," he said, and continued walking like Chester in Gunsmoke. "I'm just stiff," he said. "Homer's the one who's in the best shape around here."

This is a story to demonstrate that: See? Why stand worrying at the front door when everything can just as easily come in the back? In fact, Why worry? We're all like little baby stock markets, some days we're up, some days we're down. Best to wake up each day and look up, look down, look all around and then say, "Ah. I'm still here."

Writing Tips

Occasionally I like to offer tips on writing. Here are a few: Bob Trout was a broadcast news announcer who was known for his ability to ad lib. He said he thought of the microphone as a telephone. That's a good way to write: think of the page as a telephone, just TELL somebody something, without second-guessing yourself. Believe me, there will be lots of time later to second-guess yourself. If you're lucky, a good sunset or some boysenberry pie or a trip to the drive-in movie will interrupt that second-guessing. Or blameless sleep. Or an honest conversation with someone you love.

Another tip, from Samuel Coleridge: *"I could inform the dullest author how he might write an interesting book—let him relate the events of his own life with honesty, not disguising the feelings that accompany them."*

The wonderful Geraldine Page said something about acting that's also true of writing: *"When the character uses YOU, that's when you're really cooking. You know you're in complete control, yet you get the feeling that you didn't do it. ...You don't completely understand it, and you don't have to."*

Here's one from Eudora Welty: *"Making pictures of people in all sorts of situations, I learned that every feeling waits upon its gesture, and I had to be prepared to recognize this moment when I saw it. These were things a story writer needed to know."*

Finally, perhaps ironically, here's one from me: If you want to fall apart as a writer, turn your head away from your own instincts and start asking everyone else what to do.

Playground Bulletin No. 3

A vignette from the land of kid-dom: I'm
walking my dogs past the playground. A ball
comes sailing over a maybe four-foot-high fence.
Immediately afterward, a kid about nine years old
comes sailing over the fence to retrieve the ball.
"Hey!" I hear his playmates say. "How'd you DO
that? How'd you jump over that FENCE?"
Though they are hidden by bushes, I see them
anyway, all of them with...oh, I don't know,
striped t-shirts and worn jeans and purple stains
around their mouths from popsicles. Crescents
of dirt above their elbows. "How'd you DO
that?" they ask again, admiring, frustrated. The
jumper raises a shoulder, his eyebrows. It is not
so much an expression of not knowing as a
gesture of pity. He picks up the ball, jumps back
over the fence, and play resumes.

Gabby

At last! A warm day! The dogs are lying outside with their eyes half closed; it's like the weather is petting them. As for we non-canines, we're taking walks and bending down to admire close up the flowers that have suddenly emerged. The kids on the playground were WILD today, tossing around balls and running hard and jumping so high it was like pogo sticks were built into their sneakers. The decibel level of their shouts and cries and laughter was impressive. Yet when the teacher blew a whistle they stopped what they were doing and came right over to more or less quietly line up. I need one of those whistles.

Gabby: What for?

Me: Never mind.

Gabby: I know what you're thinking. It won't work

Writing Ideas

A lot of writers get asked where ideas come from. For many of us, the answer is, "Beats me." I was just coming up the stairs with the laundry basket and some voice whispered in my ear: *Remember Billy Harris?*

All these years later, I still remember my un-requited love in fourth grade, he with every strand of hair Brylcreemed into place, he with his swell brown leather belt, he who read aloud so well in reading circle. And I remember all the other boyfriends, too. I remember the ones who broke my heart, and the ones whose hearts I broke. (Frank, who was my boyfriend when I was a senior in high school, and loved Tony Bennett, sent me a poem he wrote in the mail that I still have, and proposed to me standing on a curb so he would at last be taller than I. "Will you marry me?" he asked. And I, astonished, said, "….No!" And he said, "Why not?" And I said, "Because I don't love you." And he said, "Oh.")

I'm always struck by what people remember most about old loves, by which memories stay and stay. Lying on the sofa with someone and listening to "The Way You Look Tonight" over and over. Staying out all night at the edge of the Mississippi River to watch the sun come up. Taking a spontaneous road trip in an old, old truck and singing show tunes as the miles flew past.

So this is where ideas come from, sometimes. Laundry baskets.

Gracie

Gracie is my cat. I got her from a farm in Wisconsin.

Me: Gracie! What are you DOing????

Gracie: Lying here. Duh.

Me: Get off that robe! That's a gift for my mom! Get off!

Gracie: [stares imperiously, and flicks tail]

Me: Get OFF! Bad cat!

Gracie: Bad cat??? BAD CAT?? Oh, this is hysterical. I will get off because I'm going to the laughatorium. But before I go, just one little thing: this is not a robe. It's my new bed. Because I want it to be.

Me: Didn't I tell you to look for mice in the basement?

Gracie: Yeah, you told me to do that.

Me: And?????

Gracie: Oh, hon. I hope someone gives you a book about cats for Christmas.

Describe Yourself in 50 Words or Less

Describe yourself in 50 words or less, is what the "question" was. Here is my answer: It is snowing, has been all day. I decided that if I did a good job shoveling, I could have some hot chocolate with lots of marshmallows. But then I just had the hot chocolate and didn't shovel at all.

Christmas Lights

I have made some Christmas cookies and done an awful lot of "testing" of them. I have found a cache of vintage Christmas cards and I love to read the verses. Here's an example:

> *A Christmas wish*
> *for happiness*
> *That's most sincere and true*
> *And through*
> *a Happy New Year*
> *May all go well with you.*

I examine each signature, done so neatly and with a fountain pen. I wonder about those people's lives: Edna Wilkes. Clara M. Felch. Robert and Richard Hirsch. Charlene Jean Lucas. George and Francis. The Barnetts. Auntie Calvert. Mr. and Mrs. Harold L. Grimpa. Recently, my friend Bill and I were driving through a not exclusive neighborhood, a poor neighborhood, I would have to say, and I was struck with the number of houses that had lights out, festive decorations of all kinds. Some of the houses had a LOT of lights. I said to Bill, "You know, I'll bet those people's electric bills go way up from those lights."

"Yup," he said.

"And it's all for anyone who just happens by. They don't even see those lights from inside their house."

"Right," he said.

I thought that most, if not all, of those people put up those lights with such good will. And that in these times good will is so rare and needed. For me, this is why Christmas time is still good. That, and this incident, which happened yesterday. Bill had just walked the dogs in 2,000 degrees below zero weather. When he came in, I said, "Open your mouth and close your eyes and you will get a big surprise." So he did that and I popped a Russian teacake in his mouth and he spoke around it to say, "Umm, dars grod." Then we went to the movies downtown where there were more decorations, which I stared at and stared at and stared at with a little smile on my face that would not go away.

 Gabby

Gabby: Excuse me. It's Saturday. The day is fine.

Me: I know. Just a minute.

Gabby: What are you DOING on that computer all the time?

Me: Earning a LIVING. So that you can have chicken TENDERS on your DOGFOOD.

Gabby: Okay, see? That was a test. Because you don't only work. You look at recipes. And real estate. And clothes. And shoes. And you stare for ten thousand hours at photos of your grandchildren. Who are not as cute as I am, I don't care what you say. Also sometimes you just sit there, doing nothing.

Me: Noooo, that's when I'm writing. Sometimes I just sit there but I'm not just sitting there. I'm seeing things. I'm hearing dialogue.

Gabby: You know, you said you were going to have oatmeal for breakfast and you had a big fat piece of cinnamon toast. I saw you.

Me: What does that have to do with what we were talking about?

Gabby: I'm a dog. I talk. You want logic, too? Now, listen: it's Saturday. The day is fine.

Me: Okay. Okay. Okay. Go and put your leash on.

Gabby: I have to do everything around here.

Look at Me!

I know you're supposed to promote yourself as an author, especially these days, but I have to tell you, every time I post something in that vein I feel like the time I was a little kid (probably dressed in my cowgirl outfit) and stood outside my house yelling, "Mom! Mom! Mom! Mom!" When she finally stuck her head out of one of the upstairs windows and said, "WHAT?" I said, "Look at ME!" And then...just...stood there.

Hummingbird

One winter, I had the wisdom to live in California
for the winter. One of the things I loved most
was the great number of birds I got to watch.
Oftentimes I had my doors open, and sometimes
a bird would fly in. So one day I look over and
there's a hummingbird on my sofa. He's just
sitting there, his wings stretched out, as though
he's at an ornithological Tupperware party waiting
for his mixed berry punch to be served to him. I
move slowly toward him...get closer...he keeps
sitting there. He's cocking his head, looking
around with his beady little eyes. I have a dog in
the house I'm worried about hurting him and I
say quietly, "You'd better go back outside. Go on,
now!" I wave my hand a little. He sits there. I try
to put a piece of newspaper under him to scoop
him up, he sits there. Gabby becomes aware of
him. "Don't you dare!" I say. And then I implore
the hummingbird again to go back outside, but he
won't. So I very gently wrap him in a dishcloth
and put him out on the deck. He's not moving
much. I check on him a little while later and his
wings are still stretched out; he hasn't moved at
all.

 After a few minutes, I go back out and his
feet have fallen into the cracks between the
boards of the deck and his eyes are half closed.
The wind blows and the force moves his head;
he's really weak. I go in the house and tell Gabby,
"I don't think he's going to make it," and I think
we both feel terrible. Then I get the

hummingbird feeder and hold it up to him to see if he'll drink. Nope. I put it right up to his beak and dribble a few drops in. He makes the tiniest movement. I try it again, and again. Then once more. Not much response. I think, *Well, you're not going to die on a splintery old deck. You're going to die in the soft green grass, by the jasmine, in the sunshine.*

I carry him down the steps and lay him in the grass, on a paper towel. I sit down by him so he won't be alone when he dies. Then his eyes open and he starts looking around. Moves his wings. And then, after a few minutes, he takes off and flies up into a nearby tree. I hear a little peep. "You're welcome!" I say and I'm smiling all the way up the stairs and into my house.

Writing Process

Whenever I do interviews—as I did yesterday in advance of the Santa Barbara Writers' conference—and someone asks about my writing process, I find it difficult to answer. It's not a process; it's how you are. I truly do believe that writers are born, not made. If you're a writer, you're a person with a habit of noticing, of being totally captivated by events as small as the sideways drift of falling leaves, or by the guy who tosses pizza dough up into the air, or by a woman in a kerchief waiting for a bus. You have a need to translate what moves you or angers you or inspires you or mystifies you into words, into stories that make a point you can't make any other way. You use what you write to explain the world to yourself. Writing happens at the keyboard or on the page, yes. So often, though, it also happens when you're pulling weeds or watching the slow flap of a new butterfly's wings or tossing cheese into your grocery cart or taking a shower. If you're a writer, you sort of never stop working. You're like a magpie, always keeping an eye out for the glittering thing to bring back to the nest.

Sentimental

When I first started sending things out for publication, I would stand at the mailbox with a submission in my hand, both reluctant and eager to drop it into the slot. It meant too much to me. What I wanted was to do in my writing was to touch someone in the way that I myself had been touched. It reminds me of something a friend's young son once told him, when he gave his Dad a lick of his ice cream cone: "I hope you taste it the same as me."

More than twenty-five years later, my sentiments are exactly the same: I still want to give to a reader what is in my heart. If that's sentimental (a word that these days is tantamount to saying "cockroach"), so be it. After all, as David Foster Wallace so beautifully put it:

"Postmodern irony and cynicism's become an end in itself, a measure of hip sophistication and literary savvy. Few artists dare to try to talk about ways of working toward redeeming what's wrong, because they'll look sentimental and naive to all the weary ironists. Irony's gone from being liberating to enslaving. ...The postmodern founders' patricidal work was great, but patricide produces orphans, and no amount of revelry can make up for the fact that writers my age have been literary orphans."

Tiny Dares

Last night I joined a bunch of women for singing. So much fun, all of us in our straight-backed chairs, gathered around the piano, harmonizing. The group was started by a woman who asked herself a very important question, one that all of us should ask ourselves more often: *Why not?* Why not start a musical group out of all your friends who like to sing? Why not offer an unexpected compliment? Why not pick up the tab for an unsuspecting couple at the local diner? And so on. I think it's accurate to say that the best things in my life have come from taking myself up on tiny dares.

Frog Story

My daughter Julie just called and told me this story: Her six-year-old son and five-year-old daughter were playing with their stuffed animal frogs, and the frogs decided maybe they should get married. But then Matthew's frog expressed some doubt, saying, "I don't know if we can stay together forEVER..." Katie's frog was silent for a long moment, then asked, in her high, pretend voice, "Is it because we have different habitats?"

Exit Row

You know how when you sit in the exit row, the flight attendant asks if you're able/willing, etc.? And you say yes but you have no idea what you're able or willing to do because you have not, as instructed, familiarized yourself with the safety information card? Because if there's an INCI-DENT, what, you're going to be in charge? No, I don't think so. You're going to be screaming or praying and squeezing your neighbor's hand. Or, if you're me, you're going to be thinking of a way to conceal your purse as you exit the flaming aircraft because, if you survive, you will need your phone and who knows, maybe your Visa card. Well, today the flight attendant asked the people in the exit row the usual question and THEN she said, "Okay, so how do you open the door?" Yes!! She gave them a quiz!!! One man bravely ventured, "Um....you pull the lever?" The flight attendant just barely kept from rolling her eyes, but you could tell she wanted to, and then she launched into a very long explanation about how to open the door, how much it weighs (just so you know what to expect when you heroically toss it aside and let others exit before you, I guess) and THEN she showed the exit row people a medical kit and gave them detailed information about THAT. At last the day has come when I am thrilled NOT be in the exit row.

Poems for Sale

So here's the best thing that happened at the South Dakota Book Festival I just attended: After I had finished all my work, I went down to the bar with some other women for a drink. At the table next to us were a bunch of poets. My friend Fee asked them to say a poem for us.

"How much will you pay us?" they asked.

"How good are your poems?" asked we.

We put some money on the table, which felt swell; I felt like a cowboy in a poker game, my hat way back on my head, my chair tipped back on its legs. One by one, three poets came to stand before us and recite a poem, and they were all wonderful. Truly. We applauded and told them to take the money.

"No, no; it's free," one woman said and they all went back to their table. But not long after, they sent over a representative who said, "We're going to take the money after all." My theory is that after they read, they came up with this haiku:

We must be stupid.
We passed up money for drinks.
Someone go get it.

Miss Hornbuckle

For me, September will always evoke pencil boxes and white paper with red margins and blue lines and new shoes that felt like straightjackets to feet that had been barefoot most of the summer. It also makes me recall my abject fear of Miss Hornbuckle, the meanest teacher I ever had. Everyone was afraid of her, even if she wasn't his or her teacher. Once I had to throw up and I went up to her desk to seek permission to go to the bathroom. She ignored me for a while—which she often did when a student asked her for anything, it was a matter of principle with her. When she finally turned to me, I said in a tremulous voice, "Miss Hornbuckle, may I go to the restroom? I feel sick to my stomach." She looked out over the room and said, "CLASS, IF EVER YOU HAVE TO THROW UP, FOR HEAVEN'S SAKE JUST <u>GO</u>."

I ran out into the hall but didn't quite make it to the bathroom. The janitor had to clean up after me and he was such a nice guy about it. He smiled and waved away my apologies. All I wanted to do was spend the rest of the day with him. His cart smelled like floor wax, a lovely scent. He wore a soft tan uniform. He spoke Spanish. And his eyes were full of kindness. Miss Hornbuckle's beady eyes were full of daggers and disgust. Thank goodness I had a lot of wonderful teachers to make up for her. Mr. Lyons, for example, who, once you proved to him that you knew the rules of capitalization, did not require you to use it in your creative writing. And if there was anything that made me feel cool, it was using no caps. That and dirty dancing, but that's another story for a different time.

State Fair

Just back from the Minnesota State Fair and am writing with arm extensions so I can reach the keyboard over my belly. Let me just say this: funnel cakes with extra powdered sugar. Corn dogs with the mustard drawn on in a wavy line just so. Hot roast beef sandwich and mashed potatoes. Corn roast more than once. Those little donuts. Martha's chocolate chip cookies. Cheese curds. Strawberry shortcake. Caramel apple. When I went into the swine barn to see the baby pigs, one looked up and said, "...Mommy?"

The Grand Farewell

Some people climb to the top of the highest
mountains or see the Taj Mahal or do any given
number of things that become peak moments.
For me, there is this: I was leaving Boston yesterday afternoon to fly home to Chicago. I had gone
to visit my daughter and her family, and as I
walked toward the cab, blowing kisses to my four
year old granddaughter who was standing
barefoot on the lawn, watching me go, she bent
from the waist to offer this: "Goodbyyye! I'll
NEVER FORGET YOU!!"

Autumn Joy

Just back from a walk and this is what I saw: half a block ahead, a kid about eight years old, lying flat out on the sidewalk. At first, I though, Oh no, is he hurt? and I quickened my pace. But he wasn't hurt. He was taking in this glorious warm fall day, one of the few we'll have left. He was looking at the blue sky and the leaves on the trees—mostly green, but some turned orange or red or yellow. He was taking it all in, and he just had to lie down to do it right. I almost joined him but instead I only smiled when I passed by him. He was getting up by then, his backpack slung over one shoulder, joy in his eyes. He smiled back in that way that is a high five in a glance.

The Visitor

This morning, I told myself to be on the straight and narrow because I ate so much last night. Breakfast? A half cup of Cheerios with sliced peaches. Lunch? One third of a chocolate pudding pie covered with whipped cream, which I had after the devil knocked at my door and I let him in and hung his coat and made him comfortable in my kitchen. "How ARE you, Satan?" I asked. "How's business?" He waved his hand. "Acht! I can hardly keep up." Then, with a burning gaze: "Eat the rest of the pie." "Okay," said I. Happily, I'm afraid. After a nap, I'm going to the willpower store.

Spring Peas

I finally got my tomatoes in yesterday. Two tomato plants, as well as a basil plant and a green pepper plant. You would think I had created heaven and earth. I woke up this morning dying to go outside and see the plants, as though something spectacular might have happened overnight.

I used to have a friend who lived in a house he built with his own hands. He had a lot of land, and he had a lot of animals, and he had a magnificent garden. When the peas first came out in the garden, he used to write me a letter and I would drive from Boston to New Hampshire to visit him, so we could squat in the garden and eat those peas right off the vine. One time, his cocker spaniel had had puppies, and after we ate peas, we played with the puppies. They lurched about unsteadily and tumbled over each other in play and my friend and I both laughed when they growled. It's been over thirty-five years since that day, and I've never had a better time. Nor do I expect to. So often, you don't know, when you're in the middle of doing something, that it will turn out to be one of your best memories. But I knew it that day. I knew it and so did he. I could tell by the way he looked over at me, the sun in his eyes making him squint, his smile brilliant and shy. A shy smile is a sight to behold on the face of a man who's over fifty. He started to say something, then just shook his head. I smiled back at him, and nodded.

On the Roof

I was puttering in my garden and Buddy, the guy who was working on the house next door, leaned over the fence and we talked for a while.   I said, "It's hotter than hell out here," and he said, "Yeah, come up on the *roof* with me!" He's repairing gutters up there. "Sure, I'll be right up there," I said, and we laughed. Then I went into my air-conditioned house where I put away the groceries I'd just bought, groceries of summer: red, yellow and green peppers, hummus and baba ganoush, pineapple, cheese, sliced chicken breast, spinach and lettuce and a big bouquet of all-white flowers for my study, where I should be working right now. But all I wanted to do was go outside and climb that tall, tall ladder in the heat and humidity and learn how to put up gutters and wear red suspenders and a white straw hat like Buddy was wearing. He knows how to fix/build/ design EVERYTHING. I so admire that. When we were talking, I told him we should have martinis on the porch come sundown, and then I remembered that I had dinner plans and he remembered he had to repair some kitchen cabinets for friends whose dogs ate off the corners. (Gabby: Who is that dog? I'd like to date him.) Drinks another time, Buddy and I agreed. Oh, but I itched to climb that ladder and sweat hard like him. What is summer for? I might go and buy a kiddie pool and then climb that ladder and after a few hours of grueling work, invite Buddy into the pool for lemonade martinis. More likely I'll just stay in my air-conditioned house and every now and then look out the window at Buddy on the ladder and sigh.

Dessert

Bill and I went out to dinner the other night and when I'd finished my quite delicious fish, I told Bill that I really, really wanted a little bit of a dessert made with peaches and blueberries. "Get it!" he said. (This is one reason why Bill is such a good friend.)

So when the waitress came, I said, "Do you have a dessert made with peaches and blueberries?"

"No," she said.

See? This is why I write fiction. Then I get to make the waitress say, "Well, hon, of *course* we do. What kind of a restaurant would we be if we didn't have a dessert with peaches and blue-berries in the summer? I'll bring you some right out."

Bad Haircuts

I'm getting my hair cut today. Why oh why am I this old and still afraid of my hairdresser? I make chit chat like I'm totally relaxed but beneath the plastic cape my hands are clenched and I'm watching those scissors like a hawk. And why? What am I going to say if it appears the cut is going all wrong? Nothing, that's what. And what does it matter in the grand scheme of things? When I think of bad haircuts, or potentially bad haircuts, I'm always reminded of a neighbor I had in San Francisco when I was 25 years old. She got a really bad haircut one day and she came to my apartment and she was practically howling she was crying so hard. Then she abruptly stopped crying and said, "Gosh. I'm so glad I'm already *married*!"

Front Porch No. 1

I have always maintained that I must live somewhere where there are seasons. If you don't endure
the howling winds of winter, how can you fully
take in a pleasant summer day? This weekend, I sat
out on my front porch reading *Consequences* by
Penelope Lively and enjoying the little breeze that
came up every now and then and prevented it
from being too hot. I ate one white chocolate
truffle, then two, damn it. I watched people go by:
joggers, women friends walking together, tourists
who come here to look at the Frank Lloyd
architecture in the neighborhood. I saw three little
girls riding bikes and they were playing some kind
of game where the lead rider was saying, "The
King! The King!" and the other two were pedaling
quickly behind her, one saying "He's coming! He's
coming!" in an English accent whereupon the
third little girl said, "Wait. Are you French?"

Fireflies

I have been so deeply appreciative of summer these last few days. Last night I went out onto my back deck and saw many, many fireflies in the garden, like miniature Japanese lanterns. And I just stood stock still in my pajamas and watched. My VW beetle was parked in the driveway, and the little red security light was flashing on and off and a firefly kept circling around the car window, in love, I thought, with that racy <u>red</u> firefly. I thought, why don't I just sleep out here? Last night Bill and I took a walk in the dark and I was looking at all the fireflies and telling him how much I love them. "What are they, though?" he asked (Oh, I love it when he treats me like Mr. Wizard), and I said they were actually rather ugly insects (beetles, as it happens) which is kind of disappointing when you want them to look like Tinkerbelle, as I do. But no, there they are with their multiple legs and antennae. One similarity between Tinkerbelle and fireflies is that they are both trying to attract love objects, but the fireflies have the wisdom to go after someone their own size.

Two Hearts

My grandson, Matthew, is 18 months and seems thrilled with his sister. He drags his little stepstool over to Katelyn's daybed so that he can stand on it and stare at her. He pats the top of her head, very gently, like she is his very own puppy. But his mother and my daughter, Julie, told me that he saw her kissing Katelyn the other day and he simply froze and stared. She said he didn't seem hurt, or angry, just sort of puzzled that someone else would get the kind of affection and attention that he gets. She said it just killed her. I know what she means. I remember after my second was born, I was weeping in my hospital bed because I just didn't see how I could love TWO children. I told the nurse that my mind kept boinging back and forth between the two girls; I couldn't focus on one without feeling bad about the other. The nurse said, "Oh, honey, soon you'll just think of them as 'the kids.'" I told Julie this story, and I told her she'd find that her love was not divided, but doubled. "I know," she said. "It's like you grow a second heart."

Halloween

Okay, it's happened. I am officially a crabby old lady. Yesterday was Halloween. I always used to like Halloween. I liked it especially when I was a kid, of course. I wore a homemade costume, stayed out until I couldn't carry my overloaded candy bag anymore, came home and stuffed myself, then put the leftover candy under my mattress and ate one piece a night in the dark after I'd gone to bed, very satisfying.

As an adult, I used to like to open the door with my golden, Toby, dressed in his Halloween costume, which I made for him (oh, the happy hours I used to spend leafing through Butterick and McCalls and Vogue pattern books). He was a clown and wore a polka dotted ruffle around his neck and a cone hat with a pompom on the top, and a harlequin patterned body jacket. I would hand out candy while Toby was admired for his get-up.

But yesterday I was in a bad mood and thinking thoughts like this: Oh, nobody makes costumes anymore, they're all store bought. Too many parents come along with the kids, so that when you open the door, it's like a PTA meeting. Big kids (like age 17) come and hulk on the porch wearing no costume at all, just demanding candy in their silent way. And my new dog, Homer—I am very sorry to report this, but it's true—my new dog, who was rescued from a home where he was abused, cannot be trusted not to bite little kids and he gets very excited every time the doorbell rings and barks nonstop.

All things considered, I decided to pass on Halloween. I put out all the candy with a note that said, "Please do not ring the doorbell. And please take only two and leave some for the others. Happy Halloween!" What a dumb note. What it really said is, "Here. Take the damn candy and get lost. I hate Halloween."

After I put the candy out, I sat in the kitchen, hiding. Soon, I heard footsteps on the porch and then I heard a high little voice reading my dumb sign aloud, and I wanted to go and see her costume but it seemed like it was too late. But it wasn't! I should have run out onto the porch and ripped up the sign, saying, *Ha, ha, ha, only kidding, wasn't that a stupid joke, only kidding, let me see your costume, turn around so I can see the back and the sides, too, oh, hooray, hooray, great costume, Happy Halloween, take another candy, take two more, take a whole bunch!* But I did not do that and then it really did seem that it was too late, I had sealed my own fate and I sat at the kitchen table and then I moved upstairs to hide in my bedroom and read the beautiful poetry of Marie Howe and looked out the window onto the street below at all the little kids, wildly excited and running from house to house. Though, after a while, they did not run to my house, because (just to complete my awfulness) I also had not turned the porch light on. I stood and watched those kids go by and I thought to myself that next year I am wearing a costume and so is Homer (his costume will be devil horns and a muzzle) and I will answer the door with gusto and hand out FULL SIZE SNICKERS.

Birthday Blueprint

I am back from attending my grandson's second birthday party, and I have seen the light. I, who have always detested and lived in fear of parties, now have a blueprint. If you want to have a terrific party, follow these rules:

1. Decorate the party space using a jungle theme, and include a monkey hanging from the chandelier and a lion stuck up on the ceiling.

2. Provide guests with big people food (baked brie with fig jam) and kid food (pizza and a jungle cake in the flavors of both chocolate and vanilla).

3. Invite one guest. One. Do not worry when he sits in the booster seat beside you looking awfully vague.

4. For entertainment run around and around the house strumming your play guitar and singing "Happy Birthday to Me." Alternate this with running around and around and around the house pushing your bubble-making lawn mower. Occasionally stop and point to the bottom of the thing and explain to any guest nearby, "Bubbles come out."

5. After partying for about an hour, tell your guests you're going upstairs to take a nap. Then immediately do precisely that.

My next birthday, I know exactly what to do.

A Summer's Evening

Today I was in town doing some errands and I saw an older woman walking slowly along the sidewalk, holding onto her caretaker's hand. The older woman said brightly, "Do you know what day it is? It's July 28th!"

"Yes," her caretaker said. "I know."

"Well yes," the woman said, "but it's July 28, 2008."

"Yes," her caretaker said. "I know."

Well, I didn't know! I mean I kind of knew it was July 28th; certainly I knew it was getting to the end of July, but I knew it only abstractly because my head is always so full of this and that and my mind is always chattering away about not much. But when I heard the woman say that, I was kind of shocked. The 28th of July! Suddenly so far into the summer! And I've only seen the ice cream truck three or four times, driving around playing those tinkly songs!

I read a column recently where the writer suggested those ice cream trucks drive way too fast, and I think the author was right. Bill said when the ice cream truck used to come through his neighborhood it just crawled along. That way all the kids could have time to run in and beg money from their parents for a Nutty Buddy. And then they could get all sticky so they'd have a worthwhile project in the bathtub later on.

But anyway, that woman's comment about what day it was probably contributed to what I decided to do tonight, which was to wander slowly and aimlessly about. So after I ate a dinner of leftovers, I set out. (I don't know why some people don't like leftovers. Whenever I eat leftovers, I feel like I'm getting away with something, and I really like feeling like I'm getting away with something. Plus the food often tastes even better than it did the first time around.)

I walked past gardens and it was the time of night when the white flowers just glowed. I went past the library and all the lights were on and looked so welcoming, so what could I do, I went in to have a look around. I wandered around the fiction stacks, and found Henry James's *The Portrait of a Lady* and sat and read it for a while and it was really fine. I thought, I need to read only classics in the summer. I wanted to check the book out but I didn't have my library card, so maybe I'll go and get it tomorrow. It had a nice size print and the pages felt soft and buttery like they'd been turned by hundreds of hands.

Then I walked some more, past people wheeling little kids in strollers, past couples eating ice cream, past joggers, past groups of teenagers looking cool and tough, past the interior design studio with all the intriguing stuff in the window, past the park where little kids and big kids were swinging in the dark, past the coffee shop with people sitting at the little round tables earnestly talking. When I came home, I sat on the porch and thought that the older lady I saw earlier today might already be in bed and asleep, but I kind of hoped she wasn't. I kind of hoped she was sitting out in a lawn chair, taking in the summer night herself, maybe pointing toward some summer constellation with a steady hand so her caretaker might see it, too.

Rainy Day

A cloudy day, and rain seems imminent. From the time I was a little girl, I have looked upon rainy days as being the best ones to give over to reading. I like the darkness necessitating a reading lamp, the sound of the raindrops pattering against the windows and coming down harder on the roof, the puddles on the sidewalk creating bathtubs for the birds. Today, thanks to an essay by Christopher Borrelli in the *Chicago Tribune*, I intend to revisit Joseph Mitchell, who, along with E.B.White, wrote some of the best essays I've ever read. In a review of his collection, *Up in the Old Hotel*, Verlyn Klinkenborg in "The New York Times Book Review" wrote of Mitchell: *"He himself remains...a melancholy man, wandering with a sandwich in his pocket among the wildflowers in abandoned cemeteries, seeking the company of solitary men who are gregarious only in the company of other isolates."*

As a writer, people often ask me who my influences are, and I always say nobody, that I just like to do my own work in my own corner of the sandbox. But I have to say that I am greatly inspired by writers like these who believe, as I do, that there is nothing at all ordinary about ordinary life. It seems to me that the lessons I need to keep learning are how to bring true and ongoing compassion to myself and others; and how to really see everything nature (and in that I include human nature) offers. And then to celebrate that. If I have a mission as a writer, that's it.

Front Porch No. 2

Last night I lay on the wicker sofa on my front porch listening to the little girls across the street crying over and over, "WATer! Twenty-five CENts!" At one point one of the girls said, "WAter! Twenty-nine CENts!" and her business partner admonished her, saying, "It's twenty-FIVE!" and the girl laughed and said "Oh, yeah." Total sales during the time I was out there? Zero. But the water business occupied itself with cartwheels and speculation as to what else they might add to their inventory. One idea they had? Caviar.

60

I'll be sixty years old on Tuesday. I feel like I've
been out in the gulley where I used to play as a
little girl and I came in the house for a drink of
water and my mom said, "Oh, hi. You're sixty."

Dinner Party

I had a dinner party the other night and was a nervous wreck beforehand even though I had decided to make food I was COMPLETELY COMFORTABLE with. Food is like a horse; if it senses you're nervous, it will misbehave.

"It's going to be retro night!" I had gaily told my guests, and so I made butternut squash soup, little individual BBQ-lemon meatloaves, mashed potatoes, green beans, and an apple pie. But when I checked on the baking pie, I saw the top crust separating from the bottom and juice running out all over the place. I thought, *What the.....???* and then realized I'd forgotten to put in the flour as a thickener.

I called my friend Phyllis (whom I'd already called in a panic about how much cheese to buy for appetizers and how long to wait to serve dinner after the guests arrive and why do people have dinner parties anyway when it makes you such a nervous wreck), and she answered by saying, "*Now* what?" I told her that I'd screwed up the pie and that also I didn't have a big enough tablecloth and so had covered the table with a bunch of *en pointe* vintage tablecloths.

"That sounds great," she said.

"Really?" I said.

And she said "Yeah!"

"Can you come over?" I said in my little voice that I use when I'm feeling sorry for myself.

"I wish I could," she said, in her soothing, motherly voice that she uses when she wants to sound soothing and motherly.

I said I'd been going to make another pie but damn it, I didn't WANT to, so I decided that I would just admit to my guests that I'd made a mistake and we'd have to eat the pie with spoons. Or, I said, I would tell them it was a fancy FRENCH version of an apple pie, MEANT to be very, very juicy and eaten with spoons, *Apple Pie de Plus Juice Napoleon.*

"Oh, don't lie," Phyllis said. "They might know you're lying."

"Oh, they'll *definitely* know I'm lying," I said. "But see, that will be part of the entertainment portion of the evening. But maybe when I serve the pie, I'll say, 'You know, there's a tradition in quilting where you always leave a mistake in the quilt, because life isn't perfect. But it's still good. And there's a mistake in this pie, but I'm going to serve it anyway, because you all are my friends and I feel safe with you.'"

"Yeah!" Phyllis said, and again I asked her to come over and again she said no (she does live in California, after all), and then we hung up.

Well, when it was time to serve the pie, I said my little speech and then guess what? THE PIE WAS FINE. I don't know how that happened and I choose to think it was a miracle.

Oklahoma?

Eeeyikes, it's COLD. My heat is set at 70 downstairs, and the actual temperature is 62. Frost on the windows so you can't see out. Drafts coming in from here, there and everywhere. My dog, Homer, is lying right in front of the back door, where it's *really* drafty. "Are you nuts?" I asked him this morning, when I came downstairs and found him there. The other day, when it wasn't much warmer, Bill, my neighbor Bob and I had an impromptu meeting in the driveway.

"Are you ready to move yet?" I asked Bob, who had just finished snow-blowing both his and my driveway. (BLESS YOU, SAINT BOB!)

"Why *do* we live here?" Bob asked.

"Okay, so...California?" I said.

"Nah, earthquakes and fire."

"Florida?"

"Too humid."

"How about Oregon?"

"Too rainy."

"Well, where then?"

"I don't know, Oklahoma?"

"*Oklahoma!* What do you know about *Oklahoma*?"

"Isn't it warm there?" he asked.

"Well, I lived there," I said, with great authority, but then I kind of ran out of things to say. The truth is that all I remember about Oklahoma (I was nine when I lived in Lawton) is red dirt and that we ate our lunch in our classroom and that I had a crush on a boy named Wayne whom I kissed through a glass door. The original safe sex.

The Bigger Picture

When I take Homer on his usual walk, there are
two little dogs that always bark ferociously at him
and occasionally break out of their fenced yard
and attack him. They're small guys, terriers, and
very annoying, but they don't usually pose much
of a threat to my much larger Golden. The other
day, though, the dogs were loose in their front
yard and they came after Homer, and a lengthy
dogfight ensued. The owner of the little dogs was
asking if I could pull my (leashed) dog away,
which I was trying to do, and I was thinking, I
should pull *my* dog away? *You* should keep *your*
dogs contained! But no harm seemed to be done,
and I walked away, only to have the little dogs run
up and attack my dog yet again. This time the
owner and I separated the dogs pretty quickly, but
I felt compelled to say, "You know, this is the
third or fourth time your dogs have attacked
mine." I wanted her to apologize and to assure
me that she would take steps to prevent this from
happening again. But what she said was, "Yeah,
it's funny, they get along fine with most dogs, but
some dogs they just don't like." I fumed for a
while and then kind of forgot about it.

In the next couple of days, Homer began
licking at a certain spot and it turned out he had a
wound on his back leg. Then the wound got
worse. On Sunday, it was looking even worse
and on Monday morning I brought him to the
vet where he was shaved, cleaned up, given a
cortisone shot and antibiotics and one of those

lampshade things to wear around his neck. On the way home from the vet, I told Bill, "I want to stop at that woman's house and give her the bill. I think she should pay it." Bill agreed.

When we got to the woman's house, I rang the bell, reminded her of the incident, and told her I thought she should pay the bill. "Okay," she said, and then asked me to wait while she made a copy of the bill. She was gone for a long time, and I was thinking, I'll bet she's calling her husband to see if he agrees that she should tell me to take a flying leap. But when she came back to the door, she said she was going to be in mediation for her divorce all morning, but she'd take care of this. Then I felt terrible. I said, "I'm sorry. I just really wanted you to keep your dogs contained." She nodded and closed the door.

When I got back in the car, I told Bill, "Well, that's that. She won't pay the bill and I don't really care. I think she got the message. Now I just feel bad for her." But I felt bad for Homer, too, who lay on the kitchen floor looking miserable, and wouldn't eat.

Later that afternoon, the doorbell rang and the woman was there with an envelope for me with a check in it. "Better cash this fast," she said, and then added something about what had happened at her mediation.

"You know what?" I said. "I don't want the money. I just want your dogs to stop trying to kill my dog." I invited her in, and she saw Homer's lampshade and awful wound and began petting and sympathizing with him.

She said there were two dogs on my block that always attack *her* dogs. So we kind of laughingly agreed to stay off each other's blocks. Then we started talking about how terrible you feel when you're getting a divorce, and I said, "I'll bet when this is all over, your life will be much better."

"That's what everybody tells me," she said, but she looked doubtful. "I'm putting my Mom in a nursing home this week, too," she said, and then I REALLY felt bad for her. We talked a little more and then she tried to give me the money again and I said no, keep it.

When the woman was going out the door, she said, "Nice to meet you, though I'm sorry we had to meet under these circumstances." I said, "Nice to meet you, too."

Later, I told Bill this story, and he said, "What was her name?" And I laughed and said, "Oh good grief, I never asked." But I do know her name. It's my name and your name. Because everybody can have something bad happen that doesn't really represent them, and it's not always that we get a chance to have someone see the bigger picture. I'm glad the woman and I got to see each other's. Oh, and Homer is fine. He's eating and playing ball as well as he can with a lampshade on his head. This morning, he chased a squirrel and clanged into the fence with no ill effect whatsoever.

A Gift

This morning when I stepped out of my front door to get the newspaper, there on the porch, to my immediate left, was a baby bird. At least I think he was a baby. He wasn't all fuzzy and fledging-like; he was just a tiny, tiny bird with orange feet and toes so thin they looked like pieces of thread. He held so still, didn't blink, didn't seem at all flustered.

"Hey," I said. "What are you doing here? Did you fall out of the nest?" Not a move. And then I thought, Wait, is this a statue? A little figurine? I moved toward him and then he *did* move. He got a little nervous and hopped a little ways away. But not far, as though what he really wanted to do was stay.

I thought, Oh boy, a gift from heaven, someone sent me a bird and he's *beautiful,* he's like nothing I've ever seen, he is mossy green gray with wonderful round eyes and thread feet, and I'm keeping him. And I will always tell the story of how I found him and everyone will think it was a miracle, which it was. And then I thought, but wait, what does he eat, does he eat worms? And I got very unhappy because I don't really like touching worms. We had to *dissect* a worm in Mr. Weaver's seventh grade science class and I was all creeped out until I learned that worms have seven hearts—seven aortic arches, to be more accurate—and then I was grudgingly admiring. But still, I don't like touching worms. They actually do feel like what you fear snakes will feel like, but then you find out that snakes feel dry as a Coty compact.

But anyway, I thought, well, maybe I can feed him raw hamburger. And then I thought of how I'd probably have to keep him in a cage if for no other reason than protection: I might step on him, or the cat or dog might eat him just for fun. And I thought of how if he were in a cage he wouldn't see the clouds move across the sky and the raindrops hanging from the leaves and the stars at night and the rabbits who hold so very still when a dog goes by. And so, reluctantly, I tossed a little towel over him and put him in the garden in the middle of some lovely purple flowers that grow under the weeping cherry and he hopped farther away. I hope he's okay. I like to think he's still my pet, but with a VERY large cage.

Dusk

Once, out for a walk at dusk in the country, I watched as the sky turned a deep, smoky red before darkness fell. Then, in the velvety blackness of a warm summer night, I saw a huge field full of fireflies, rolling acres being lit up here, there, everywhere. I was filled with such gratitude; I didn't know what to do. I stood still at the side of the road, little white wildflowers still visible in the dimness, the smell of grass and trees and earth in the air, night clouds drifting by. My hands felt too big at my sides, and my heart felt stretched. I thought, I wish I could stay here forever, but then I ended up staying for only about seven minutes before I walked home to change into pajamas and read. What a funny species we are.

As for now, I'm thinking a fragrant, lukewarm bath is in order. Then reading. I wish I could read by fireflies, like I did as a little girl one summer night. I loved it. The fireflies did not, I think I am safe in saying. I let them all go the next morning and not a one of them looked back and said, "Hey, thanks for the hospitality. Loved the holes you punched in the jar lid."

Looking Out and In

It's a cloudy day, humidity thick in the air, and it's almost foggy. Good vampire weather, if they didn't sleep during the day. When do they ever get to the post office, is my question? Wet leaves are pasted to the sidewalk, and from my office window I can see changes on my service berry tree: orange touches here and there, as though it has been to the beauty parlor to be highlighted. Kids are back in school, and one of my favorite things to do when I walk Homer past the elementary school at the end of my block is peek in the windows so I can see what all the kids are up to, to see how the teachers have decorated their classrooms. I once wanted to be a teacher, but I fear it was mostly so that I could wear high heels and lipstick and decorate bulletin boards.

Confessional

People say that envy is a poisonous thing, but if you ask me, it's regret that causes the most damage. If you've done something wrong, intentionally or not, it's in the past and you can't undo it. All you can do is apologize, attempt reform, and move on. Easy to say and so hard to do. In my experience, regret is like the gnat of emotions: swat it away, and here it comes back again.

One can brood far too much over mistakes; one can even have one's life consumed by them. Notice how I use "one" rather than "I". Let's be honest, here. I brood too much on mistakes, and I do feel sometimes that my life is consumed by them.

So it is that I was particularly appreciative of today's email from Eknath Easwaran and the Blue Mountain Center of Meditation. These daily emails start with a quote, and this was today's, by Saint Teresa of Avila: *"It is here, my daughters, that love is to be found, not hidden away in corners but in the midst of occasions of sin."*

This quote inspired a little vision in my head. A woman is in a confessional, overcome by guilt and grief and sorrow. She is wearing a dark cloth coat and a thin kerchief over her hair, the colors faded. Her head is bowed, as, in fact, it usually is. She whispers her sins to the priest, who is seen only as a dark profile. She lists her sins and lists them and lists them. Finally, she has finished, and she waits to hear what her penance will be. It will be substantial, she thinks. Her soul is black, she thinks. Corroded. What happens, though, is that the priest only whispers back to her, "Me, too." And the woman's soul turns white and then it is a bird, and it flies her right out of that confessional and into a bakery, where she buys a caramel roll and coffee for herself, and she whispers to the person behind the counter that she would like her card to be charged for whatever the person behind her orders.

This seems to me to be a perfect penance. A perfect penance and a perfect celebration. Maybe the two are oddly linked, and always have been.

Welcome to the World!

The other day, I saw some blue balloons waving in front of a house in my neighborhood.

"Did somebody have a baby boy?" I asked Bill.

"I think so," he said. "The woman in that house was pregnant."

The next day, I looked out my window and there was the woman standing in her front yard holding a tiny baby and bouncing him up and down in the time-honored way.

"Oh! Oh! I'm going to make them some cookies!" I told Bill.

"That would be nice," he said.

So I made some chocolate chip cookies and put them in a container and taped a card on top. I left the cookies on the front porch by the door and I did not ring the doorbell because here's what I know is going on in that house: F-A-T-I-G-U-E.

I don't know the names of any of the people in the house, so I put "To the newest member of the neighborhood" on the card, and inside I wrote, "Welcome to the world!" I told the baby to tell his parents to enjoy the cookies—WHICH HAVE NUTS!—I warned. And then I worried that the mother was nursing and couldn't have chocolate and only her husband would eat the cookies (right in front of her, no doubt), although maybe that no-chocolate-for-nursing-mothers rule has fallen out of favor. I hope it's fallen out of favor; nursing mothers need chocolate just like the rest of us. But more than the nuts or the chocolate, I worried about gaily writing "Welcome to the world!"

In 1975, when my first daughter was born, the news came on the TV in the hospital one morning, and I burst into tears. What kind of savage place was I subjecting this innocent little girl to? What kind of dangers would she face in her life, and not only in her life, but in this very day that lay ahead of us?

Those times seem awfully tame compared to what's going on in the world now. In addition to that, there are plenty of people who take exception to celebrating the birth of yet another human being on an already overcrowded planet. But I can't help it. I never can help it. There are those little hands, and there are those feet, and there are those searching, brand new eyes, and there is ....what? Hope. Possibility. I see a flailing newborn's arm as though he's waving an invisible victory flag.

You know, I learned last night that the three most commonly translated sentences on an iPhone are: How are you? Thank you, and I love you. I guess I want to say that to every baby I see. Or hear about.

Good Kids

Yesterday, I went to work—in Austin, Texas. I got up at six a.m., fed the dog and the cat, drank coffee, and packed: a little make-up, and some books to read on the 8:30 a.m. flight. I had such a good time reading on the plane, I didn't even mind sitting in a seat designed for Thumbelina. I used to love flying but now it has become like riding Greyhound bus without the possibility of weird but wondrous adventures.

One good thing that happened on the airplane is that on the first leg on the trip home, I got to sit in front of a bunch of boys who were on an Indianapolis high school's swim and diving team. There were boys and girls on the team, there were a whole bunch of them all dressed up in their red-and-white team sweats, and I noticed that the boys and the girls were NOT MIXING AT ALL. I thought, how can that be? How can there be a group of adolescent boys and girls who are not flirting like crazy, if not stealing off to shadowy corners for some serious making out? I decided it was their coach, who, in advance of them traveling together, had said LISTEN. THE SPORT COMES FIRST. JUST FORGET THAT YOU HAVE HORMONES. IF YOU REMEMBER THAT YOU HAVE HORMONES—AND I THINK YOU KNOW WHAT I MEAN—IF YOU REMEMBER THAT YOU HAVE HORMONES AND YOU ACT ACCORDINGLY, I WILL TRACK YOU DOWN AND HURT YOU BAD. I AM

SERIOUS. YOU THINK I'M JUST BEING COACHY, BUT I'M BEING SERIOUS. These kids were also amazingly polite.

We all had to change planes in Dallas/Ft. Worth, which is a HUGE airport, and we stood together waiting for the train—the "Skylink" (don't you love that name, you just feel like you're in Disneyland)—to take us to another terminal. Just before the train arrived, this auto-voice (a female auto-voice, one of those sterilized voices stripped of all personality whatsoever, when, if they want people to listen, they should use someone like Louis Armstrong or Tom Waits or Sarah Vowell) came on, suggesting that passengers waiting for the train not get in the way of those disembarking. Well. The train arrived, the doors opened, and one of the Indianapolis swim team girls immediately started to get in the train. And one of the Indianapolis swim team boys said, "Jessica! Are you serious???" "What?" said Jessica, and she stopped in her tracks, all embarrassed. "Did you not hear the announcement??" said the boy.

Oh, it was so sweet and rare and that is why this afternoon I'm going to move to Indianapolis, land of incredibly well-behaved and, gosh, really good-looking kids. I thought of turning around and telling the boys who sat behind me on the airplane—all of whom were sort of ridiculously handsome—that when I was their age I was afraid of boys, especially cute ones, and never knew how to behave around them and what do boys want, anyway?

It seems to me that Freud was a dope. It's easy to understand what women want from men. Strength and vulnerability, duh. But what do boys want from girls? Besides the obvious. Or IS it only the obvious? So I gathered my courage and turned around but then all I asked is, "Did you guys compete in Austin?" Yeah, they said. "How'd you do?" I asked. And they started nodding their heads and they said, "Good, we did good." And I smiled and said, "Good for you."

I eavesdropped on them all the way home. Here is what they talked about: how big dogs are better than little dogs, and how Golden Retrievers are especially awesome. College, in general and also in particular because they were worried about the choice a friend of theirs was making. A YouTube video about the Snugly, which this parody had renamed the "What the f#$% blanket." How far sports stadiums are from city centers, how that distance varies, city to city. When the flight attendant came around with the drink cart, they said both "please" and "thank you." Kudos to their parents.

Gabby

Gabby: Hey! Hey! Did I hear something about a new dog park? Were you talking about that?

Me: Yup. There's a new dog park coming. It has seven acres.

Gabby: Really? Can we move there?

Me: Well, we can go there a lot.

Gabby: How many hours a day?

Me: Um. One?

Gabby: ONE?

Me: I...you know, have to work.

Gabby: BRING your work!

Me: That's an idea. Except in winter.

Gabby: What's wrong with winter?

Me: Too cold to be out long.

Gabby: Jeez. Your designer must have been tired or something when he made you. So what does the dog park have?

Me: Land. Lots of land. And I think there's a place where you can get water.

Gabby: That's it? No meat locker or anything?

Me: No. Just land, so you can run full out.

Gabby: Okay, I'll take it. I happen to know there's a hot dog stand nearby. A Portillos.

Me: How do you know that?

Gabby: Never mind. I know where all the hot dog
         stands are. You could take me through the
         drive-in on the way home. You know how
         everyone dies of cuteness when dogs go
         through drive-in restaurants and they get
         something, too.

Me: Well, yes. They get a biscuit, usually.

Gabby: You know how you're always talking about
         how to make the world a better place.

Me: Yeah.

Gabby: Get me a hot dog. That's one way. No
         mustard, extra meat, extra bun.

*I understand millions have been clamoring for my photo. Well,
here I am. Despite the way this looks, I do not have three legs.
One leg is stylishly tucked under me. I am lost in contemplation,
as you can see, thinking about Plato and the third law of
thermodynamics. Also about how good sausages are.*

Church Shopping

Last weekend, I visited three churches. I was raised Catholic, converted to Judaism, and now consider myself a Pantheist. My places of worship can range from the local coffee shop to a playground where kids tear around or stand solemnly contemplating something, or simply to a state of mind caused by seeing great art, for example, or reading poetry so powerful it's like a sock in the stomach, or witnessing a tender exchange between people that makes you believe we are not such savages after all. But I have begun feeling the need for ritual in my life. So I went to see what I might see.

On Saturday evening, I visited a Catholic church that still offers its masses in Latin. I sat in the back, hearing those familiar sounds, watching the priest in his white vestments with the gold trim, remembering how, as a little girl, I used to envy priests their wardrobes and how it always seemed so strange to see their black and clunky men's shoes poking out from under their chasuble—shouldn't it be something a little more formal? White satin wingtips, perhaps?

I looked around at the little crowd of people who had come to this mass, maybe twenty souls spread out among the pews, and I saw that the women all had something over their heads, in one case, a lace mantilla that looked very beautiful. I had nothing on my head and felt a little ashamed of myself. I remembered when women who had forgotten hats used to bobby-pin Kleenex on top of their heads, but I couldn't bring myself to do that, even though I always carry a lovely hankie in my purse and COULD have used that. But no, I sat there with no hat and with jeans on beneath my coat. Black jeans, though, that could have passed for pants.

There was no sermon, which was an unexpected bonus. Not that there can't be inspirational sermons, but there was something nice about sitting in a beautiful place, all wood and stained glass, hearing only the lovely cadences of an ancient language, the words echoing over a sparse but mostly devout audience—judging by the bowed heads, and the way you could practically feel the intensity of some of those people in prayer. *Dominus vobiscum*, the priest said, and I remembered sitting next to my father in church, regarding his large hands, wondering what he was thinking, because I had a suspicion he was not paying so very much attention to the service.

Nor was I, obviously.

Communion was given the old way, with people kneeling at the altar and NOT TOUCHING anything, but instead tilting their heads back to receive the host upon their tongue, while the altar boy held a gold platter beneath their chin, lest something fall. And I remembered when you used to have to fast before you took communion; nothing could be in your stomach when you received the host (how vile the notion of eggs and bacon sloshing around inside one's stomach when God himself arrived!). Once someone in my church fainted. It happened up in the balcony, remember when churches used to be so crowded, even up in the balconies? There was the loud noise of her falling over and then a lot of high and feminine expressions of alarm and concern. The fainter was a large woman, overweight, I suppose you would have to say, but she was very beautiful: black hair, red lips, all very Liz Taylor-ish, in my opinion. And she just conked out, and I thought it was very dramatic and wonderful, once I realized she was all right and just hungry. She was wearing all black, I remember, and her velvet hat had a gorgeous veil. We are poorer for not seeing hats with veils much anymore.

Anyway. I went out into the night after that mass and I felt lighter in spirit, and a kind of peace had taken up residence at my center. I think it's because no matter what kind of service you attend, you are coming together with other people to address a shared need for something spiritual that cannot be gotten in our day-to-day, normal lives.

The next day, Sunday, I went to a Quaker service that was held at an arts center. There were folding chairs set up in a room that seemed to be a store. Various things made by artists were being offered for sale: things painted or knitted or cast in metal. I had to work hard at not looking at those things and concentrating instead on what value sitting in silence can bring. For that is of course mostly what happens at a Quaker service, is that you sit in silence. So I stared at my lap and then I closed my eyes, and I felt the richness of a shared silence, which is very different from silence you experience alone. Someone would sniff or cough now and then, or shift their weight in their chair, but these sounds just seemed to pass though the room, and were not distracting. You are allowed to speak at a Quaker service, should the spirit move you, but 45 minutes passed before anyone offered any words and all, and the time just flew by. It was like bathing in peace. When a man finally did speak, I opened my eyes to listen, and I looked at the expressions on people's faces. One woman looked like a toddler who woke up a little out of sorts. One looked radiant, and another simple confused.

After the man spoke, it was time for the service to be over and for everyone to share, but I had to go because I was on the way to the next church, which, as opposed to the other services I attended, was very well attended. It was in a big fancy church, well appointed, a huge bouquet of flowers at the altar. I sat in the back, which is a popular place for parents with babies to sit, and so I was well entertained by the wide eyes of this baby resting against his mother's shoulder or that toddler crawling on the red carpet, playing with his blue car and his blocks. There were candles lit on the altar, including one for Advent, and the sight was lovely to behold. But I could not respond to the sermon, because it felt to me like too much of a performance. As though the person delivering it was thinking the whole time, Man, I'm good. Truth be told, I found the service a little boring. But then I thought to myself: You critical person. You just sit right there. Don't you move. You listen to the end, because you might miss the whole point here, and you might be entirely wrong about this being "boring." Don't you move a muscle. So I sat there until the end but it didn't get better so I flirted with the toddler and after the sermon I listened to the choir sing one song and then I started thinking about how the Pancake House had pigs in a blanket and then I just shot out of there and went to the Pancake House where I had....guess what?

A Promise

When I was a nurse, I once took care of a patient who was dying from an illness related to cigarette smoking. I remember a particularly poignant day when one of his relatives brought him a new bathrobe. He looked splendid in it—it matched his bright blue eyes—but he told me he knew he wouldn't be able to wear it for long, and he was right. The bathrobe went home with his relatives after he died, draped over the arm of a grieving niece, and I remember thinking, I hope she wears it. I hope she puts it on and thinks of him. I liked this man a lot, and I used to sit beside his bed and talk to him whenever I could.

Those were the days when nurses actually had time to talk to patients, which is one of the most important and therapeutic things you can do, but there is hardly ever time for that now. But don't let's go there today. Let's go there another day, when I talk about how nurses used to give back rubs and change linens twice a day, which was also important. And how I used to make gold stars to tape above the beds of the patients after they passed gas after surgery (important indicator of a patent system!)

Anyway, one day near the end, this patient asked me to make a promise to him. He asked me to tell every person I saw smoking, to stop. He said, "Tell them what happened to me. Tell them they don't believe that smoking will hurt them, but it most likely will." Shortly after he died, I came upon a group of teenage girls smoking. And I gathered up my courage and went over to them and said, "Excuse me. I'm doing a favor for a friend." And then I told them about the guy, and they exchanged glances with one other and refrained from telling me to stick it. But that's what they were thinking, I could see it in their eyes. And if someone had come up to me when I was a teenaged girl and told me to stop something I was doing, I would have had the same reaction. I never again told anyone else this patient's story; I never suggested to anyone else that they stop smoking on his behalf. But every time I see someone smoking, I think about him. It's been nearly forty years, now, but I always think of him, sitting there in a blue robe he would wear for far too short a time, asking me to ask others to honor his request. Ah well. That's the nature of human beings. You can't usually stop them from doing something they want to do, even if it hurts them. Sometimes even especially then.

Spring Cleaning

I have been inspired by my daughter, Julie, to do a little spring cleaning—she's doing it with a vengeance. Inspired by her and something else, I should say: the fact that I could not find my angel food cake pan this morning and tried a creative alternative that means I will be scraping sticky black stuff from my oven for some time. When I was searching for the pan, I found some tiny pie tins I had forgotten all about and now will use the next time I make dinner for friends: I'll make individual blueberry pies. I also found a whole bunch of Tupperware I'd forgotten about too, or else why JUST YESTERDAY would I have bought a whole bunch of Tupperware? Well, it wasn't Tupperware. Where can you get Tupperware anymore? And I really like Tupperware, too. I like that there used to be Tupperware parties where a saleswoman in a pastel colored shirtwaist dress demonstrated the Tupperware burp. You'd have dainty girl food and then come home with, oh, lettuce keepers and popsicle makers and something to tote cakes in.

But this got me going, this discovery of the leftover containers and the tiny pie plates. So I started rummaging around here and there and in my bedroom I found photos of my grandchildren that I've been meaning to place in scrapbooks for years, a huge pile of photos. I found books I want to read. There were things to discover and appreciate anew in every room in my house: cool rubber stamps and ink pads in funky colors, lovely barrettes that were shoved out of sight in the back of a bathroom vanity drawer, letters I've saved to read again, exotic spices. And then I began to see things I have not seen for a long time, even though I walk past them every day: the Parisian gaming table I HAD to have and as soon as I got, ignored. The orchid I was so delighted by that I got up early to say hello to it the morning after I bought it, then failed to notice again. The painting I bought by a man who was also a poet: an evocative image of a path between trees that I told myself I'd meditate in front of. Right. I dug through my pile of CDs and listened to Melody Gardot, then Johnny Mercer, then a collection of Doo-Wop. You know, we complain all the time that kids just end up ignoring the fancy toys we buy them. But we ignore our toys, too. So this afternoon, I'm planning to sit at the dining room table with a cup of tea, piles of photos, and the time to look at each image before I place it.

Spring

Spring is like living inside a poem: The lilacs really ARE wet with rain, and the air really IS perfumed, and it really is mudilicious. I love walking around the neighborhood at this time of year, looking at all the gardens. Today I saw a rosebush on a boulevard, a corner garden. It was not planted where anyone who lived in the house it was in front of could see it easily. It was an act of such generosity, to put a rosebush where only passers-by could see it. I stood there nearly misty-eyed and then Homer took a whiz on the bush. So much for thinking that everyone must feel the same way about things that you do. I also saw a bird high up in a tree today just singing his heart out. Wouldn't stop. A man who was walking toward me and I just stood there and watched for a while, then smiled at each other and kept walking. It was a nice moment. The buds for blossoms are still tight on some trees and they remind me of lipsticks rolled up partway. The sky is cloudless and that impossible blue, the kind of sky you wish you could wrap up and save in a box under your bed. All hope is here. That's what spring always feels like to me.

Gracie

I notice I say everything twice to my dog (e.g. "Good MORNING, boo-boo! Good MORNING! Are you a good boy? Huh? Are you a good boy?") but not to my cat. I wonder why that is.

Gracie: Because we get it the first time around? As opposed to The Unfortunates?

Liable or Not Liable

I did a television interview for *The Last Time I Saw You* today. I almost went to an electric company rather than the TV station, but otherwise things went well. The best thing that happened in the TV station is that the news director's assistant came in the green room and told me she had read my book in an afternoon.

"You know what always happens when I read your books?" she asked. "I want to be a better person."

"I want to be a better person, too," I said. "But I never am."

"Me either!" she said happily.

After the interview I went to court to try to get out of a ticket I'd been given for backing into a parking place in a municipal lot.

"How do you plead?" the judge asked. "Liable or not liable?"

"Not liable," I said. And I told her how when I pulled in there was a car directly across from me that had also backed in and that the sign that said not to do that was obscured.

She said, "I agree with you. I've been to that lot and the sign is obscured."

Well, with that, I was kind of feeling like we were new BFF, and I said, "Can I just ask, on behalf of others, that you make that sign easier to see?" Then she got mad and told me she had nothing to do with that and if I wanted to tell someone else, fine, but all she was responsible for was forgiving my fine. So I slunk out of court, a little embarrassed but twenty dollars richer. A fair trade.

Lemonade Stand

On Thursday morning, I looked out my window and saw that the little girls across the street had set up a lemonade stand. Oh, boy, I thought. I'm going to buy some, later. I'm going to buy two glasses of it—or two paper cups, more likely.

They had a little white table, and they sat professionally behind it on two little white chairs. Being stationed in the middle of the block and without benefit of any advertising that I could see, business was not exactly brisk. I watched them for a while, sitting there waiting, perhaps dreaming about what they'd do with the fortune they expected to make; and then I went to work.

By the time I looked up, many hours had gone by, it was early evening, and it was time to take the dog for a walk. And after that, I needed to do a million other things. So it was with some haste that I snapped Homer's leash on him and started off down the sidewalk.

"Want to buy some lemonade?" one of the tow-headed entrepreneurs called out from across the street.

I did want to. I had promised myself I would. But now there was the beating of that drum in my head: hurry, hurry, hurry.

"Sorry, not right now," I called back.

"Okay," the girl said. "Well, have a nice day."

"Thank you," I called back, feeling like the old lady who yells at kids who get balls on her lawn.

"Are you going to be there tomorrow?" I asked.

"YES!" she said, jumping up and down a little.

"Okay!" I said and I thought, Okay, tomorrow I will definitely buy some lemonade.

The next day was so hot the heat index was something like 113 degrees. But when I looked out my window, there was the little table, all set up on the sidewalk again. There was a pink construction paper sign in the shape of a heart taped to the table, fluttering in the breeze, but I couldn't read the message on it. I saw that the proprietors were up on the porch in the shade, where they could see customers without subjecting themselves to the brutal heat, and I figured the sign said something like if you were interested in lemonade, approach the girls on the porch and they would happily serve you. Serious inquires only, it might say.

When it was time to walk Homer, I looked in my wallet. All I had was a ten, and I thought to give it them and if they couldn't make change, well, I'd tell them to keep it. Then I decided ten dollars was too much, it might make them uncomfortable. Five, okay. But ten? A little weird. So I found four quarters and put them in my pocket and I headed across the street.

When I got to the little table, I was happy to see that lemonade was 50 cents. Perfect! But there was no sign of the girls. A new construction paper sign, this one in yellow, said, CLOSED. But below that, it said, "We'll be right back." But they never came back. And I felt disproportionately sad. Why? Because there was such hope in that little girl's voice when she asked if I'd like to buy some lemonade. Because the girls' signs were homemade, from colorful construction paper, and

I was pretty sure they'd had quite a conference about what color the signs should be, what shape. Because every day those kids grow older and soon the coltish, messy haired little girls that they are now will have morphed into teenaged girls who wouldn't be caught dead selling lemonade, who would understand instantly that the gain would never equal the effort. But for every single one of us adults who walked or drove by or, best of all, stopped by that lemonade stand, the gain was immeasurable. Easily worth ten bucks, for the way it brought back memories, or demonstrated that kids are still kids in the Andy Griffith way some of us remember. It's worth ten bucks to see a kid with a purple plastic headband pour you a drink from a plastic pitcher so heavy for her it wobbles dangerously when she pours, the same kid who entertains herself by turning cartwheels between customers. Some kids are using their imaginations and getting good ideas and turning them into reality. I've learned my lesson; I'm ready to do my part.

It won't be today. Today is going to be more severe thundershowers, as there was last night. I woke up this morning to a flooded basement, and Bill uncomplainingly helped me bail out.

"You're going to get such a good dinner for this!" I shouted to him over the roar of the shop vac.

And he will get a good dinner. When Bill first showed up to help, I was standing by the garage where I'd gone to get the shop vac. I was ankle deep in water and the yard was a virtual lake. It was pretty grim. But the first deep blue morning glory had opened up on the vine I planted to grow up the garage.

"Hey, Bill," I said, pointing to the blossom. "Life, huh?" He nodded appreciatively and then squared his jaw for work, and so did I.

Good Question

I got a letter from a girl who's doing a school project about me. She had just a few questions. Number one was: What makes you tick?

Thanksgiving

I told my friend Phyllis that I love Thanksgiving, that I have never had a bad Thanksgiving. Being the natural optimist and sunny personality that she is, Phyllis said, "You've got to have had at least one bad one. THINK!"

The Mystery

I read a quote today by Judith Butler that says, *"We're undone by each other. And if we're not, we're missing something. One does not always stay intact."* I have been feeling not quite intact lately, because of...oh, a lot of reasons, and it will not surprise you to learn that as a writer, my way of dealing with it is to write about it. Since I was a child, I have found consolation in writing; more importantly, I have found truth.

Yesterday, I got a call from a very good friend who, knowing I'm going through a tough time after a death in the family, among other things, suggested I write something happy.

Not my style. I told my friend that when I was diagnosed with cancer (I'm fine now), I kept waking up in the night. My doctor wanted me to take a pill to help me sleep, but I wanted to keep waking up in the night. I wanted to respect the process I was going through, to learn what I needed to learn and come out the other side. I think that to deny your feelings about something is only to make them stronger. To deny your feelings also takes a terrible toll on you, and often on those whom you love and who love you.

Tonight I am going to a Taize service, which I love for its candlelight and music and lack of somebody trying to tell you What It Is. Because nobody knows what it is. I like to sit amongst people who recognize the mystery and celebrate the fact that it is a mystery.

The Good Old Days

Memorial Day weekend is coming up, and I really want to go to a family picnic and eat burnt hot dogs and burnt marshmallows, both roasted on a stick. When I was a kid, I used to go to our family's annual Fourth of July picnic. I ran around in a towel and bathing suit and jumped in and out of the pool and in addition to the hot dogs and marshmallows, ate plenty of other delicious things that the women had brought and put down on oilcloth tablecloths: macaroni and potato salads, my mom's oatmeal cake with boiled brown sugar frosting, ham and turkey and baked beans.

That was a time when I really felt a whole day, start to finish. We'd get to the park early so as to secure a good spot; and we'd leave late at night after the fireworks were done, happily worn out, our nose and shoulders burned by the sun, our hair smelling of chlorine.

I used to like to watch the division of labor: my dad and my uncles manning the grill and drinking Hamms beer, grouped in loose circles as they talked about manly things. My mom and my aunts sat at the picnic table in their shorts and tucked-in blouses and sandals (sometimes with nylon socks) supervising the kids and handing out paper plates and cups and plastic utensils. They wore sunglasses that to my child's eyes made them different people. It revealed a side of them I hadn't quite realized they had. Sunglasses on my Aunt Lala? No. More comfortable for me to think of her in her apron at the dinner table, dishing out meatloaf and admonishing her children to take their elbows off the table.

My grandparents enjoyed what seemed to me to be a kind of royal status: they sat in lawn chairs and did nothing much beyond moving their chairs so that they could stay in the shade. Though my grandfather did also listen to ball games on his pocket-sized transistor radio; he held it up to his ear and offered alternating expressions of rapture, despair, and occasionally a deep frustration that made him cry out *Cripes!* or, in more severe cases, *Jesus, Mary and Joseph!* and then look around as though the party responsible for his anguish were nearby and available for interrogation. There were so many of us then! They are all gone, now, all those aunts and uncles and grandparents, and a few cousins, too, and Memorial Day has become…well, Memorial Day.

A Recipe for Thanksgiving Leftovers Sandwich

1. Pull beleaguered turkey from refrigerator. Also pull out all the other leftovers. And the big jar of mayo.

2. Get out the icky white bread, the kind so soft it folds over in your hand before you've even *done* anything to it. Wonder Bread is best.

3. Spread both sides of the bread with a lot of mayonnaise. A *lot*. The goal here is to have mayonnaise squishing out of the sandwich every time you take a bite.

4. Pile on some turkey. Salt it.

5. Pile on some stuffing.

6. Pile on some cranberry sauce.

7. Pile on some potato chips. That's right. You don't want your chips on the side because you will get too nervous about getting the right potato chip/sandwich ratio.

8. Pile on some gravy and also some green bean bake.

9. Enlist the service of the resident strong person to help you get your masterpiece onto a plate. Keep telling that person that this is YOUR sandwich; no, they cannot have a bite, if they want one, make their own.

10. Put sandwich on the table and go and get one of those cokes in the little blue/green glass bottle. Only the little one. The little ones are best because they fit properly in the hand and they have the right amount of syrup and also they

remind you of Santa Claus whom you like even if you don't believe in him because he's s such a good guy and because old as he is—and jeez, think how OLD he is!—he still has a nice smile and a well-groomed beard and from all accounts, he treats his wife and animals very well.

11. Photograph your sandwich from a few different angles. You will use one of these photos to have a t-shirt made to sleep in and to remind you that next year you can have another sandwich just like this. Not before, or your doctor and Michele Obama will get you.

12. Take a huge bite. Chew until it's all gooshy. Then call your little grandchildren over by using a series of grunts and gestures. Lean down close to them, point to your mouth, then open it wide, When they say, EWWWWWW!, smile. Say, "War a bi?" When they say NOOOO, smile again.

13. When you have finished eating the sandwich, go to the kitchen and get out the left over pie. You know what to do.

Mirror Gazing

Last night I called a good friend and asked what she was doing. "Looking in the mirror," she said mournfully. "God, I'm getting so OLD." She launched into a description of all the things she had seen. "I mean, I'm getting jowls!" I started adding things to the litany of horrors, things I see when I look in the mirror and then we decided we shouldn't look in the mirror anymore, and we moved on to recipes. Soon we were having a wonderful time. She told me she'd grilled a peach the other day, topped it with a dab of nonfat Greek yogurt and agave nectar and almonds and it was as good as a custard peach pie. "No," I said, and she said, "Yes!" So now I'm going to have to try it tonight. I was so grateful for the change in psychic weather and I said to her, "Boy, what would we do without food?"

"Die," she said.

Front Porch No. 3

I sat on my front porch recently, realizing that I hardly ever do that, even though it's such a wonderful summer thing to do. It came to me that it's as important to "schedule" things like this as anything else. Read an hour a day. Sit on the porch on any nice summer's eve for at least half an hour.

When I sat out on the porch, I saw three teenaged girls walk by in cut-off jeans and t-shirts and flip-flops, engaged in intense conversation. For one moment, I felt again what that was like, being a teenage girl in the summer. I remembered the delicious urgency of sharing everything with my best friends, of driving through Steak'n Shake in search of a thrilling kind of romance that was never going to happen there. Or anywhere, for that matter. I saw an older man fly by on what looked like a new bicycle, and it made me want to get a new bike, too. I heard voices from near by houses floating out the screen windows, and I heard the pounding of sneakers on pavement and the short, fast exhalations of the runners. The dogs lay with their front paws hooked over the top step, panting, their ears up in the high alert position. And I thought, ah, who cares what sorrows might visit you in a day? Look out at the summer night from the chair on your porch, and be glad.

The Joy of Cookbooks

I asked a friend of mine if she would like a cookbook. I had a bag of them that I had not yet stored on my cookbook shelf.

"Nah," she said, with nary a glance into the bag.

"Why not?" I asked.

"They're not necessary," she said, and I was literally struck dumb.

Oh, I know the allure, the joy, really, of finding new recipes online, the ease with which you can compare and contrast one version of chicken enchiladas against another, or find a healthier version of a high cal, high fat recipe you love that actually tastes good, too. I know it feels good to save on paper and reduce clutter. But no cookbooks?

I visited my parents recently and for some reason my 90-year-old father and I were talking about cookbooks. I said, "Hey Dad, do you remember you gave me my very first cookbook?"

"Did I?" he asked.

"Yup," I said. "I was ten years old and we were living in Fort Hood, Texas. I was in the PX looking at a junior cookbook, and you came in the store and saw me. You asked if I wanted that cookbook. Did I! I only went and looked at it with lust in my heart nearly every day! But you bought it for me and I started cooking right away from it for you and Mom, remember?"

He shook his head, smiling. I guess he probably doesn't remember anymore. But I do. I remember lying on my bed and reading recipes for spaghetti and meatballs, for French toast, for jam-filled muffins. And every recipe began with the same first instruction: "Wash your hands." Good advice for me, a kid who loved being outside, the closer to dirt the better. That cookbook also showed you how to set a nice table, how to fold a napkin beside a fork, so that you communicated the fact that your guest was not only welcome but esteemed at your table.

I got *The Joy of Cooking* for a Christmas present from my ex-husband when he was just my boyfriend and we were living in a dump of an apartment. We never had any money; I was a nurse's aide and he drove a cab and once we had a screaming knockdown over what to spend a single dollar bill on—it was all we had left until payday, and payday was a long way away. But. I found the recipe for Brownies Cockaigne in that cookbook and I bought the best ingredients I could find and I made the brownies and I was absolutely astounded at how good they were. And the smell! Reader, I put them in my car and drove around with them so I could continue to smell them as I ran errands.

As a young mother, I checked out *The New York Times Regional Cookbook* and Dinah Shore's cookbook and copied recipes out onto index cards. When I joined Weight Watchers, I bought armloads of cookbooks in an effort to not feel deprived. I still use many of those recipes even when I'm not dieting.

The best thing about cookbooks is the accidental discoveries you make: running across a recipe you've never made or maybe even heard of and thinking, hmmmmmm..... And then you might make it and voila: a new favorite. I found Chicken Al'alba that way, a wonderful dish for company, as they say. I found burgundy berry pie and caramel apple pie. I love the Caesar salad recipe I stumbled across in the *Joy of Cooking*; it's still the only one I use.

I even like the splatters and spills you find on the pages of cookbooks. Want to know what recipes a cook really likes? Look for those splatters. If you look in the margins of my cookbooks, you'll also find phone numbers and reminders for things to do that day. Also, a letter grade will often be written by recipes I've tried. A few recipes have this grade: A++++++. But occasionally, you see this for a "grade": NO.

People's preferences in cookbooks can let you know who they are. You've got your Giada fans and your Cooks Illustrated fans and your Ina Garten and Rick Bayless fans, to name but a few.

Sometimes, you can get a sense of who the author really is when you use a cookbook. The gold standard is Ann Hodgman, who offers laugh-out-loud commentary in all her fabulous cookbooks. But even the little individual comments in church cookbooks put together by groups of people for fundraisers are little windows to people's personalities: I particularly like the ones that sound like parts of letters from your Aunt Myrtle: Made this for my daughter's birthday, and heavens, was it tasty.

I don't know. Call me old fashioned. I am old fashioned. I always like the feel of a real book in my hand. And cookbooks are no exception. When you've had a hard day and can't face another challenge to your brain, can't even face reading from a novel you are loving because you're too out of gas, pick up a cookbook. Look at the lovely photos and read the descriptions. Eat with your eyes. Smell with your imagination. You'll go to sleep happy, and if you're lucky, popovers will show up in your dreams.

Three-Foot Instructors

A gray day here. Summer is still in the air like the faint scent of perfume after the wearer has just left the room. Fall is on the way and I can't help but be excited, even though I hate being cold and complain about being cold more than anyone I know. But you know how it goes: here come the store displays of cozy, autumn-colored sweaters and here come the school supplies and the yellow buses trundling down streets where fallen leaves are already starting to collect at the curb. Recipes for stews and soups and roasts and muffins abound, and classes are offered in practically anything you would want. The serious books come out. As do the afghans that you can lie under while you read them.

I am working on a novel where part of the "research" involves going to the library for children's story hour, and I submit to you that the way to save the world might be for everyone to go to such a thing on a regular basis. What hope is contained there, what innocence, what sly humor, what openness, what exuberance!

And something else, too. Last time I went, the librarian offered a hug from a stuffed animal—a brown bear, as it happened—and I think just about every kid leaped up to get one. They waited in line—courteously, expectantly, and seemed to give their whole heart over to the bear that they seemed to believe was real.

There is something that can happen to us, as we get older: we can develop a kind of reticence, even fear, around the notions of love and vulnerability. We can become cynical; we can fall victim to a great variety of bad experiences, we can suffer heartbreak so severe it makes us feel nailed to the floor. But here are three-feet-high instructors, reminding us of the bolstering purity and satisfaction in admitting what we need to take and to give.

Grateful

You know how it is. A million things to do, and the dogs need walking. So, I leash them up and start up the block and I am not in a very good mood. Rather, I am preoccupied and in a hurry. Homer, my older guy (12 year old Golden), stops to sniff EVERYTHING, and my impatience mounts.

"Come ON," I say, but I say it quietly, and I don't pull on his leash because...well, because he's an old guy. So we're at the playground and he's sniffing and sniffing away at something and I look at my watch and then I look up. The sky is a middle blue, and there are red berries hanging from a tree and the contrast is lovely, red berries against a blue sky. Then, because I have been given a dose of medication by Mother Nature, I slow down inside, and I have a look around. There are big fuzzy buds on some shrubs getting ready to burst open. There is a U-shaped branch of a tree that hangs low, inviting someone to sit there. There are robins scattered just so on the playing field, as though they just waiting for a robin-sized soccer ball to be tossed out. I become aware of air, of grass, of sidewalk and swings, of the sound of birds singing. And a rich content settles, and I am happy to be standing still. But then Homer has had enough and HE pulls on the leash: come on, come on, more ahead. And I follow him.

Speak of the devil. Homer just came into my study and stood looking at me. "Want to lie down on your bed?" I asked him. He looked over at it. It was across the room, and he made no move toward it. "Want to be closer?" I asked him, and moved the bed to be right behind my chair. Slowly, he moved onto it, made a circle as dogs must do before they lie down, and then collapsed on it.

"That's a good boy," I said, and ran my hand down his back and felt every vertebrae—he's lost a lot of weight and muscle mass. But here he is still, after having had a good breakfast, and in full knowledge of the fact that later, he'll go out sniffing, and I will be his grateful pupil.

Found a Penny

Sometimes I plant shiny pennies for the finding, and once I saw a little kid come upon one. He acted like he'd found the moon hidden behind the parking meter.

Acceptance

This entry was written after a repair of a retinal tear.

My vision is not so great this morning. I know that there will be some accommodation going on and this is likely nothing to worry about. After all, I saw my doctor only yesterday and our focus (so to speak) was on the recipe for the banana bread I'd brought him and his staff last week.

"I need that recipe," he said. "My wife and my daughter are all excited. Send me the recipe. And don't leave out anything. Tell me EXACTLY how you did it."

"It's just James Beard's recipe for banana bread," I said.

"Yes, but tell me everything, like did you cook it in paper? My daughter wanted to know that."

"No," I said. "I cooked it in a bread pan that I greased with a whole bunch of butter."

"Okay," he said, "Put that in there."

I adore my doctor. And he focused on the recipe, not on my eye, which he said is doing nicely, and that brought me great comfort.

Still.

This age brings a certain solemnity to one's thoughts, and from time to time one needs to sit out on the porch steps quietly, and watch the wind in the trees. One prepares, to the best of one's ability, for the inevitable difficulties and losses that lay ahead.

For me, preparation centers around the notion of acceptance, which I look upon almost as a sacrament.

By way of example, I think of a man I met in the retirement center where my parents lived. He was a minister, a really kind and brilliant man who was in the early stages of dementia. And before he told me about what was happening with him, he looked me directly in the eye and said, "I want to be honest about this."

And I wanted to lay gifts at his feet.

Journey Proud

This Friday, I go to Positano, Italy, where I'll be teaching a writing workshop and taking a cooking class, along with the rest of the participants. Cooking and writing and Italy: who could ask for more? Not me. But last night I woke up at 3am, worried about what to pack and all the other bump-in-the-night things associated with traveling, something Harper Lee referred to as "journey proud." Things like:

Missing the flight. Or catching the flight, but the flight is doomed. Somewhere over the black, endlessly deep ocean, the captain says, "Bad news from the flight deck. Apparently our wings have fallen off. Feel free to take along our complimentary in-flight magazine when you exit the aircraft."

Or: I fall asleep and start drooling and awaken to see my seatmate watching me with ill-disguised disgust. And then it turns out that my seatmate is in my writing class.

Or: I miss my connection.

Or: I get no sleep on the plane and arrive at my destination sobbing because when I don't get enough sleep I'm a mess.

Or: I lose my passport.

Or: I get sick and have to be hospitalized.

Or: My dogs get sick and have to be hospitalized.

I tried meditation. I tried my version of prayer, which is basically, "Okay, game on. Respect. Could you please help me?"

Finally, I turned on the light and Homer, who had been sleeping beside me, raised his head as if to say, "Are you kidding me?" then let if flop back down and went on dreaming his dog dreams.

I read for a while, Julie Otsuka's luminous *The Buddha in the Attic*. And my anxiety was dispelled, just like that.

I am grateful for books for many reasons, but this is perhaps their greatest triumph: they can lift you out of fear, despair, self-absorption and ignorance and put you in a place of wonder and peace. For free.

Positano

On my last day in Positano, I went with my friend Lauren and her husband Rino to Tramonti, in the hills of Amalfi, to visit a vineyard. Lauren had gotten a call that today was the day: the grapes were going to be cut. The ride up into the hills was so beautiful: look left, it's gorgeous, look right, same thing. I sat in the back seat trying to take it all in, but it's impossible; at some point, I simply turned off my mind and just watched.

A videographer who works with Lauren was waiting for us so that he could lead us to the place where the cutters were working (these grapes are cut by hand, not machine). I was struck by the pride and apparent joy of the cutters, who held bunches of green grapes up like a trophy, the sun illuminating the fruit in a way that was living art. Add to that the quite literally indescribable beauty of the hills in which the vineyard lay, and you'll have some idea of what a sensory explosion it was.

After the vineyard we visited Amalfi, and Lauren and I went to the Cathedral of Amalfi, down into the Cloister of Paradise, which is a jewel box of a place: dark, cool, rich with frescos and paintings and history. Then we had lunch at a seaside restaurant: fried zucchini blossoms, seafood pasta, fish in lemon sauce, and profiteroles limone. The food was so good; all I could do was roll my eyes and shake my head.

We ended up at Lauren's house and talked for a long time and then, for perhaps the third time, I said I really should go. I shouldered my purse and moved out onto the balcony facing the Tyrrhenian Sea and the hills of Positano, where, in the gathering darkness, the lights were beginning to come on; here, there, over there.

From the house, Lauren called out: "Rino wants to have a toast, you want to have a toast?" I took my purse off my shoulder and sat down at the outdoor table and said, "Yes!" which is really the only answer to have in Italy. Rino selected the wine, a lovely rose, then uncorked it. He set out beautiful glasses, which shone even in the darkness. Then he set about lighting candles— and stopped. The ones Lauren had put out were not to his satisfaction; he had to find prettier ones. This he did, and we sat in the candlelight drinking wine and talking, talking, talking, saying a long farewell, which is the only farewell Italians seem to know how to say. I had a sense of being there fully in the moment, but also of being in a dream. It is both, there in Positano, all the time.

A Perfect Day

I have gotten lots of wonderful Christmas presents in my life. I suppose I'm typical in remembering most strongly the gifts of childhood: the time I got what seemed like a bazillion outfits for my Ginny doll, the time I got a black velvet purse festooned with pearls, and a matching hat, which I wore with great pride to midnight mass. Also the time I was nine years old and got the teddy bear I called Hope, which I still have. But the other day I got another wonderful gift.

I awakened in the morning to the adoring gaze of my Golden, Homer, who'd gotten up on the bed during the night and was stretched out alongside me with his head on a pillow, and yes, when I opened my eyes, there his were. It made me laugh out loud, which made him thump his tail.

I came downstairs and got a cup of coffee, then went into my study to work, and it started to snow. It was the kind of snow that looked like someone had torn up lace, and it drifted down slowly and so beautifully for hours.

After I finished working, I went to our little downtown to get some shopping done, and coming down the street was a sleigh being pulled by a team of horses wearing jingle bells. The sleigh had wheels, which was a good thing, given that the snow hadn't stuck. Outside one store was a group of carolers wearing old fashioned clothes: hoop skirts and bonnets for the women, top hat and tails for the men, singing *"Fa la la la la."* And then when I emerged from another store, there was Santa, wishing me a Merry Christmas.

"Merry Christmas," I said back, shyly, and in that moment I still kind of believed in him. (I have to tell you I was devastated when I learned there was no Santa. Shattered. I remember sitting out on the curb knee to knee with my best friend Cathy, saying, "Well, maybe there's no Santa Claus, but there is definitely an Easter Bunny. No one would make that up!" She set her mouth defiantly and said, "Yeah!")

That night I went to a concert that featured singing by a choir, several sing-a-longs of popular Christmas songs, and ballet dancing by young girls wearing white tutus, a kind of personification of innocence. Even if the girls would deny being innocent, even if they would resent being called innocent, that is how they looked. There was also, wonderfully, a reading of Dylan Thomas' "A Child's Christmas in Wales." This concert was a fundraiser, and in the lobby there were gingerbread cookies lying on a paper plate, ginger men and ginger ladies, so many it looked like a small nation, and they were only five dollars for the plateful. What a deal! I bought them before the concert started and brought them in with me so they could hear too.

When I went to bed, I realized I'd had a perfect day. Joy lay on my chest like a cat. Good thing it wasn't a real cat, because it would have gotten in the way of Homer repeating his lie-on-the bed move, which he did happily that night.

Nature

A storm earlier this morning, the long rumble of thunder and the sky darkening so that the house lights needed to go on. I like witnessing the strength and variety in nature, especially when the storm passes and the birds come in droves to the serviceberry tree. They love that tree, and feast on the berries all summer with a kind of exuberance that reminds me of kids at a seasonal ice cream stand. When the birds land on the branches, it shakes loose the water that has collected on the surface of the leaves. Then there is another little rainfall, like a coda to the storm.

And now, to work. Beside me, a vase of flowers that is proving to be a bit of a distraction. I always have flowers on my desk, but these roses are reddest I've ever seen. From the time I was a little girl, I'd had a romantic yearning to be sent red roses. I was nineteen years old when it first happened, I got the long white, nearly satiny box, tied closed with a wide ribbon. And inside? A dozen deep red, long-stemmed roses, nestled in green tissue paper. They looked so beautiful lying there, I never took them out. And when they died and blackened, they were beautiful, still.

A Good Day

Today I got up and had an excellent breakfast while I listened to jazz. All you need to know about breakfast is that maple bacon was involved, which is why it was an excellent breakfast. Then I read *The Chicago Tribune*, including the business section, which I almost never read. But in this issue there was a really well-written article by Monica Phillips about a store called "Art Gecko" in the Harrison Art District of Oak Park. After I read the piece, I had to go and see the store.

On her website, artist Lisa Nordstrom says, *"I am convinced that our lives are shaped not only by the few cataclysmic events that inevitably occur during a lifetime, but quite profoundly by the collective moments of our everyday, even mundane, life experiences. It is over the course of time that we gather the memories and the pieces: the moments of comfort, pleasure, pain, loss, love, longing, sorrow and joy that truly make up our existence. It is in the spirit of gathering these separate pieces and bringing them together to form a whole that I create my art."*

She makes journals, jewelry, wall hangings that remind you of Cornell boxes. She makes Christmas tree ornaments and lamps and purses. I stayed a long time, looking at everything, and came away with a number of treasures, some of which I'll use for gifts.

When I came home, I read more of *The Cherry Pit*, a novel by Donald Harington, which is so rich and deeply intelligent, and which I am enjoying so much. I found out about this author because of another article in a newspaper

describing Harington as a vastly under-appreci-
ated writer. I had to see what all the fuss was
about. Now I know what all the fuss was about.

A third thing I found in the paper was a review
of the play *Bus Stop* which is playing in a new
theater space called The Den, at 1333 N.
Milwaukee in Chicago. I had to go, and I invited
my pal Bill to come along. I would get the tickets:
he was responsible for dinner.

Bill did a little research and we ended up eating
at a place called Mana, at 1742 W. Division
(manafoodbar.com). It was small, with a very interesting vegetarian menu, and man, was it good.
Everything was so different, which I really
appreciate when I go out to eat. I had a spinach and
pear salad with a sweet mustard vinaigrette and
mushroom sauté over polenta and a white wine
from France called La Craie. Everything was
exceptionally good. Everything. Including the
service and the bathrooms.

The day STAYED GOOD, because the play
was fantastic. A woman behind me who reviews
plays on her theater blog said afterward, "It was
so...humanistic." There's everything you could
ask for in this play: it makes you laugh hard, it
moves you, it engages you completely from the
first moment to the last. And it takes place in a
diner. I'd see anything that takes place in a diner.

Here is what I would like to do today: repeat
yesterday. Maybe I will.

Front Porch No. 4

Years ago, I heard someone suggest that he would like to go up and knock on random doors and ask whoever answered how they were doing, REALLY. That's an idea that has always appealed to me, but I think it works better in concept than in reality. For one thing, if a stranger approaches someone's front door, the person's reaction is to ignore the bell and/or hide, or open the door before the bell is rung in order to make a preemptive strike: "Not interested, sorry." Or "No time, sorry." Or "Didn't you see the NO SOLICITING sign on the door?!" The other problem is that if you ARE able to ask someone how they're doing, they usually give an answer with no more depth than, "Fine, you?" Myself included, I rush to add.

Anyway, this is a long buildup just to say that I like this page because I get to answer the question "How you doing?" more fully than usual. I have been enjoying this summer more than any I can remember, even the ones where I was a kid and ate a Nutty Buddy every single day without a thought in the world about calories and cholesterol.

Every day, I make time to sit on the front porch and read, barefoot. I keep a glass of seltzer water to my left and my dogs at my right. The dogs are very busy when they're on the porch, because they must keep an eye on all the construction workers who are tearing up the street in order to put in a new sewer line (and also try to kill the mailman, which is Homer's bad habit that he passed on to Gabby, who only goes through the motions without any real malice in her heart).

Gabby:	Uh huh, yes I do, I have malice in my heart, too, just like Homer.
Me:	No, you don't.
Gabby:	I do, I tell you!
Me:	What is malice?
Gabby:	....Is it a green for salads?

I confess that I too am fascinated by the construction. I feel I have finally connected with my inner little boy. I watch the big trucks and the little trucks and the guys running around in fluorescent vests with what I can only call awe. How do they know what they are DOing? What all is down there, beneath the streets, that we never think about? We just turn on the water and flush the toilet and that's where our thinking ends. But this! This should be a reality show!

Also in keeping with the inner little boy thing, I kind of see this all as a story playing out in a picture book, and tell myself that at night, when all of us are sleeping, the vehicles talk to each other, maybe over a cold vehicle beer. "You see that dog try to kill the mailman today?" one might ask another.

Whenever we walk the dogs down our street, I point to a little digger vehicle or a giant circle of molded concrete and ask Bill, "Hey, Bill, how much do you think that thing cost?" And he immediately gives some answer with great authority, and I say "Really? Huh!" And we both know he has NO idea.

Mostly, I'm glad I'm still curious. I think it keeps you young. As opposed to all the hairdos I looked at online today for women over fifty which declared that they made the wearer look...YOUNG!!! They were... WRONG!!! Whenever I have to get my hair cut, I look at pictures of haircuts so I can try something new and different. Then I get what I always get because I'm too nervous to change.

My Mother, Marion Jeanne Loney Hoff

Although the other entries here are placed randomly, I decided to put the following entries about my mother in one place. It just seemed right.

Recently, my 92-year-old mother was hospitalized, and often times as I sat at her bedside, I read aloud to her. Because of her macular degeneration, she can no longer read, but she listens to books on tape every night, keeping up her lifelong habit of being what I would call a MIGHTY reader. But this was daytime, in the hospital, with its hard beds and beeping machinery and humiliating patient gowns. And so we took ourselves away from that dreary environment by getting lost in a book, both of us. I looked up every now and then and saw that she was smiling, caught up in the story, and I noticed too that her roommate's noisy family quieted at one point, as though they were listening too. I felt like my wonderful fourth grade teacher (with the equally wonderful, if improbable, name of Miss Hamburger) who every morning sat on a wooden chair before the class, straightened her skirt and her eyeglasses, and proceeded to read the next chapter of a novel she was reading to us. And we all loved it: the kids who were cut-ups, the kids who got sent with some regularity to the principal's office, the shy kids like me who were otherwise slow to share their rapture.

I read aloud and the IVs dripped and the carts went by outside the room and a loudspeaker announced a code blue in radiology and babies were born and souls ascended. I thought, even here, we can be comforted and transported by words. Oh, we got interrupted a couple of times by doctor visits, by nurses tending to this thing or that, by the delivery of wan-looking meals (can't they at least put little umbrellas in the drinks, or confetti toothpicks in the bread?). But no matter how long the interruption, when we were ready to resume reading and I asked my mom if she remembered what had been going on in the book, she did. More fully, I might add, than I did.

Are Facebook "friends" really friends? I don't know, it seems like it to me. I've told you so many things that are personal, even seemingly private.

You have celebrated good things with me and consoled me about bad things. So I'm going to tell you that I've been quiet on this page because I'm in Minnesota, as my mother has been admitted to hospice care. All three of her children are here, including my brother from Hawaii, and we've had radiant experiences. Many tears, much laughter, stories told and retold, promises made.

This is a place where a white squirrel lives in the woods nearby and sometimes seems to be looking in my mother's window, where there are no "rules" that hospitals have, where my mother can wear her own clothes and have her room decorated any way she wants. Currently, it looks like a florist shop in there, and that's the way it's going to stay. People cook here all the time, and this morning the kitchen smelled like cinnamon rolls.

My mom has photos of herself and my dad, drawings by her great-grandchildren, and a bird nightlight. Today I brought her pink lipstick and two scratch-away betting cards (we won NOTH-ING) and some pussy willows, and she smiled and said, "I love pussy willows," and I said, "Me, too," and I had one of those moments I've been having a lot lately where I realized how much of her is in me, and how much I'll miss her. But you know, she had a good life, she'd be the first to tell you. And a long one! She is being given so much love right now and she is taking in every bit of it. The other day, she said, seemingly out of nowhere, "Oh, shoot!" I think it was because she was thinking that life is very beautiful right now, and she wishes she could stay around longer to enjoy it.

There is such a thing as a glorious death, and I wish that for my mom. And I hope that everything she believes is true. She has always believed in heaven, but today she said something kind of different. I had been talking about how thick the stars are in Hawaii, where my brother lives, and she said, "You know how people say that there can't be a heaven because it would be too crowded? Well, maybe when people die, they become stars, and they group together." "And talk?'" I said. And she said, "Yeah. Talk."

Okay. Back to her room. I hope I haven't made you sad. I hope that instead this will serve as inspiration for you to love all the people you love, more.

Thank you to all those who wrote to offer comfort and prayers and wisdom when my mother was admitted to hospice care. On the evening of March 15th, she was set free.

I keep thinking about a story she told me when I was a little girl and was resisting going to bed. She said that every night, fairies came into my bedroom and painted stars on my ceiling, and I'd better go to sleep so they could do their magic. I said I never saw those stars. "That's because they only paint them when you're sleeping," she said. I was plenty miffed. How could I see anything if I were sleeping? Now I'm looking at that story a whole different way.

I suppose most of us like to tell ourselves certain things when people we love die. I suppose that we allow ourselves certain fantasies, or look for great meaning in things that otherwise would be unremarkable, or interpret things in ways that let us believe our loved ones are gone on to a different, better place, or watching us, or seeing in a way they never could see before. I think it's wonderful that we do this. I think it's wonderful that we take our battered hearts and wrap them up in a blanket and rock with them for as long as it takes.

I've been in Minnesota clearing out my mom's apartment. A friend who took me to the airport yesterday asked me what things I was taking for myself. Oh, I told him, buttons from her sewing box. Her aprons. A casserole dish I remember her always making green bean bake in. Two love letters, one from my dad to her, one from her to my dad. Two spectacular photos taken of her and my dad early on in their marriage, and they radiate happiness. A tiny box with flowers painted on top. Some fancy cups and saucers. Some jewelry. Her parakeet. Her rosary. A recipe in her handwriting for her sister's Easter potatoes.

And her legacy. I want to step into her love of gardening. I want to try to learn a kind of faith she had. I want to remember and learn from the way that she found joy in the smallest things up until the very end. When she was in hospice, I had made a garden in her room: beautiful flowers and plants were lined all along one wall. I asked about them at one point and learned she could not really see them from her bed—her vision was always worse than she let on. So I brought them to her, one by one, and we admired them together and she was smiling so the whole time and cooing to those plants like they were babies. One time, I asked if she would like a little fresh air, and she said yes and my brother and sister and I opened the window for a breeze that I just like to think was created and delivered to her and her alone. She lay back and closed her eyes and she said, "Oh, the breeze."

What makes a life, if not the things we loved most in it? And I am struck over and over by the fact that it seems to be buttons and not billions that satisfy and endure.

Next weekend, I'll be going up for my final trip to empty the apartment. It will be the end of something, but it will also be Easter and spring-time, which reminds all of us, regardless of our beliefs, of rebirth and renewal and the promise of all we might not know or understand quite fully, yet live in hope of. Hope's the thing, isn't it?

When we went to the airport, my friend took not busy Snelling Avenue, but instead the winding road river road that runs by the Mississippi. And I thought about how pretty St. Paul is, and how many long years both my parents lived there. And I took such solace in understanding that they had made so many good choices, and had lived lives of such integrity and had offered to so many their love. I felt like I had so much to say suddenly, but here is what came out of my mouth: "This is a nice city."

The other day, a woman told me she was sorry to hear about my mother's death. I thanked her. And then she told me that it had been over twenty years since her mother died, and she still felt the loss. "Really?" I said. And I thought, *Oh, no.*

I think I had assigned myself an arbitrary time to grieve, and a time to stop grieving. Things are not working out quite as planned.

It feels to me now that grieving is like walking through a maze. You think you've found the way out but then you discover that you have not. You need to go back. You need to try another way. And you need—and this is very, very hard for me—to accept that you are not exactly in control of the process.

I told a friend who is on her way to see her nearly 100-year-old mother today that maybe she should give her an extra kiss when she sees her. And maybe my friend will. Maybe she won't.

If there's anything this loss has taught me, it's the lesson of not letting opportunities go by. It seems we can't help doing it, letting opportunities go by. We are programmed to think there will be another day, another time, until suddenly—and permanently—there is not. I have been spending a lot of time with guilt and regret, wondering why I didn't call to check in with my mom every day, especially after my dad died and she lived alone. I suppose I thought, *Oh, there's nothing to say, really. I'll call after a few days, when there's something to say.* But there was something to say, and it did not take the form of the words in any given conversation. Rather, it took—or could have taken—the form of my mom knowing that I cared, that I loved her, that I was just making sure she was all right. I did not do that, and my regret about it weighs so heavily on my heart. Whew, it's heavy.

I know the cure for me is time and forgiveness of self. It seems a long way off. It seems as though a maze I thought was one size has revealed itself to be much bigger and more complex.

I was out with my mom one day when I was a little girl about seven or eight, and we came upon a man begging on the street. He was a double amputee, both legs missing below the knee. I had never seen such a thing. It seemed so cruel, so absolutely incomprehensible that such a thing should be visited upon someone. Why had this happened? The man was sitting on a blanket, his pants legs neatly folded beneath his stumps. He wore tan pants, a white shirt, and a white straw hat. We walked past him and got into the car, and I burst into tears. My mother, knowing me to be the oversensitive individual that I was, wrapped some change in Kleenex, pressed it into my hand, and told me to give it to the man. I walked over to him, my face red and blotchy, and wordlessly gave him the money. He looked up at me with a glorious smile on his face—I can still see it so clearly—and said, "Thank you, little lady."

When you want to best take care of yourself, it seems the thing to do is to take care of someone else. There's the salve for today.

I woke up early today, the room still dark. I lay there for a while, thinking about how it was my birthday (mine and Ann Patchett's and George Saunders' and T.C. Boyle's, among many, many others). I felt a great sadness, and here's why: I knew that for the first time, I wouldn't be getting a card from my mom. I started to cry a little and then (I might as well confess this, as I seem to confess everything on this page) I asked for her help. I said it out loud, "Mom? Can you help?" and I felt her spirit descend and assume a kind of presence on the side of the bed, as though she had come to sit there. (After my father died, she herself used to swear she felt the side of the bed go down when he came in to be with her, so there you are. DNA.) Anyway, there she "was" sitting on the bed and here was the conversation I imagined:

Me: I'm so sad because it keeps happening, these firsts. Everybody says that you have to get past the first year, all those holidays, birthdays, but I am finding it a little harder than I thought. I think I'm okay; I think I'm resigned; but then something happens that feels.... sharp.

Mom: Well, that's how life is. Uneven. You have to just keep going.

Me: But I'm so sad that I won't get a card from you with the cramped, hard-to-read writing that you were always so embarrassed about. But I could always read it. I think we all could. I wish I had kept all the cards you sent me, but I didn't. [sniff, sniff]

Mom: You know, you have got to stop this being overly dramatic. This kind of wallowing that you do.

Me: ......!

Mom: You've been this way since you were a little girl.

Me: I know.

Mom: Well, does it help anything?

Me: No.

Mom: Plenty people have a lot of things to be sad about. I did too, in my life.

Me: I know.

Mom: But you keep going. You get up and get busy. Now, you have a lot of things to do today, don't you?

Me: Yes.

Mom: So. You get up and do them and you be of good cheer. And stop this drama. Outside, it's snowing the lacy kind of flakes I always liked best and that you like best, too. For one.

Reader, I switched a switch and got up and the snow was beautiful. I stood out on the back deck and the flakes landed on my face like a touch filled with intention. I looked up into the sky, which is also a kind of white, and I heard my mother's voice in my head saying, "I gave birth to you on this day and in so doing, gave you the world. Why would you need a card?"

I got a cup of coffee and now I'm going to sit before the window and watch it snow, and then I'm going to fill the day with pleasures. There are so many to choose from. I'd a little bit forgotten, and it's good to have been reminded. It's better than good.

I've always said that if only people at parties would talk about things like how they talk to the dead, I would like parties instead of living in fear of them. I could feel comfortable with someone who admitted they talked to the dead. Perhaps we all do that. And so perhaps I'm comfortable with everyone. At home in the world my mom gave me, after all.

Dear Reader,

I know I have already thanked you for requesting this book. Now I want to thank you for reading it. People are so busy these days, any author whose book is read should feel complimented.

I also want to take this opportunity to thank Phyllis Florin, a wonderfully talented writer and artist, for taking time away from her own work to design this book and figure out how best to publish it.

Elizabeth Berg